CRIMES AND PUNISHMENTS

Cover: Killer Clyde Barrow kneels beside a
stolen Ford, his pistols and rifle chillingly
displayed. The side of a bullet-riddled car
frames Barrow's picture.

CRIMES AND PUNISHMENTS

By the Editors of Time-Life Books

TIME-LIFE BOOKS, ALEXANDRIA, VIRGINIA

CONTENTS

1
CRIMES PERFECT AND IMPERFECT

2
GANGS AND GANGSTERS

3
INFAMOUS ACTS

4
SCHEMES AND SWINDLES

5
CRUEL AND UNUSUAL

CRIMES PERFECT AND IMPERFECT

Crime exposes the dark places in the human heart, taking their measure, gauging their depths of cunning, desperation, passion, or sheer malice. It measures, too, the criminal's urge—sometimes childlike, sometimes supremely calculating—to act with impunity, to defy the social order and get away with it.

Many of them have met their doubtful goal: burglars who cunningly covered their tracks; thieves who vanished with phantom ease; murderers who did not bother to run because they knew that the law could not convict them; psychopaths so unpredictable as to elude any restraining hand.

But the perfect crime has its polar opposite: the crime so ill-conceived, botched in execution, or undone by bad luck that it looks pitiable against the ramparts of the social order. Between the two are a thousand shadings. Yet something essential in the nature of crime is defined by extremes of outcome—the law impotent against iniquity or the law rising triumphant above a blundering foe.

Life with Mother

During his reign as emperor of Rome from AD 54 to AD 68, Nero compiled a staggering record of extravagance, debauchery, and whimsical viciousness. He stole from his subjects to finance his parties, palaces, and such personal amuse- ments as fishing with a golden net. He dressed himself in the skins of wild animals and sexually attacked men and women who were tied to stakes. And he killed almost constantly—murdering nobles for their money, poisoning an aunt, kicking a pregnant wife to death.

A central figure in Nero's life was his mother, Agrippina, a scheming and pow- erful woman who sought to control her son for her own ends and may have had an incestuous relation- ship with him. Perhaps inevitably, she became a target for Nero's homicidal urges. But getting rid of Agrippina proved a difficult busi- ness. Although details of Nero's various attempts are uncertain, he evidently tried to poison his moth- er on three occasions; but, perhaps warned by her network of spies, she always took an antidote in ad- vance. He then ordered the rigging of a device that would cause panels in the ceiling of Agrippina's bedroom to drop on her as she slept— but she discovered this plot as well. Next, Nero tried for an accidental death at sea: He had a boat built in such a way that it would collapse midvoyage. Agrip- pina was induced to travel across the Bay of Naples on the boat, but when it found- ered and sank, she swam to safety. In the end, Nero resorted to the blade: He had his mother slain with a sword and claimed her death a suicide.

Nero's murderous de- pravity—which some say included the burning of large sections of Rome that he found aesthetically of- fensive—finally triggered a revolt. When he realized he would be seized and sub- jected to grisly punish- ment, the thirty-year-old emperor plunged a knife into his throat. In the last moments of his existence, Nero tearfully mourned the world's loss: "Dead! And so great an artist." □

A marble likeness of Rome's youthful and murderous em- peror Nero survives from ancient times.

Letter Perfect

As a riveted Scottish public discovered during her murder trial in 1857, Madeleine Smith had a romantic nature, but love, it seemed, could be poisoned by mundane concerns. Whether Madeleine herself was the instrument of that poison would never be clear.

Born into a proper middle-class Glasgow family, Madeleine was living at home at the age of nineteen when she met a clerk by the name of Emile L'Angelier, of French descent and about thirty years old. Although his social position was low and his salary meager, he was an ardent fellow, and Madeleine encouraged his approaches. Their love bloomed, with the help of cooperative maids who let Emile into the Smith house when the coast was clear. He and Madeleine exchanged hundreds of letters and pledged themselves to each other.

But after about a year, a prosperous and altogether more socially acceptable neighbor named William Minnoch began courting Madeleine. Seeing that her parents favored this match and conscious that life with her present lover might be less than comfortable, she tried to break off the relationship with Emile. In response, he threatened to show her parents the steamy letters that she had written to him. He continued to visit Madeleine, but on each occasion, something in her offerings of coffee or hot chocolate left him feeling terribly ill. Emile apparently visited on the night of March 22, 1857—at least he was seen in the vicinity of the Smith home. He arrived home late that night; his landlady, noticing that he seemed quite ill, helped him to bed. He was found dead of arsenic poisoning the next morning. When the letters from Madeleine were discovered among Emile's clothes, she was brought to trial.

Letters such as these had never been aired before, and they created such a sensation that they were later published in book form for Victorian edification. In her stream of missives, Madeleine waxed effusive about every aspect of love, including sex. Although her descriptions of their dalliances were couched in the oblique style of the times, they left nothing—and everything—to the imagination, amazing and delighting onlookers in the court and mortifying members of the Smith family.

Disturbing matters of a more substantive nature also surfaced. Madeleine had purchased a large quantity of arsenic shortly before Emile died; she said she wanted it to kill rats at her parent's country house. Later, she said it was used for cosmetic purposes—a common practice at the time. But the jury and public alike saw Madeleine as an innocent, lovely Scottish lass who had been led astray by a scheming foreigner. Nor was there any evidence that Emile L'Angelier had actually visited Madeleine on the night of his death. Thus, by mental effort, it was possible to conclude that the distraught beau might have committed suicide.

Madeleine went free, but scandal had its price. Her family left Glasgow, and William Minnoch respectfully withdrew his offer of marriage. Madeleine headed for London and a life among artists, known to be a broad-minded breed. □

This envelope carried torrid evidence—one of suspect Madeleine Smith's letters to her poisoned lover.

The Making of a Legend

There are few better examples of the power of horrible crime to transform the ordinary than the story of an unremarkable, obscure, unmarried woman of thirty-two years. She lived with her father, stepmother, and sister in a clapboard home in the drab Massachusetts mill town of Fall River shortly before the turn of the century. Her name was Lizzie Borden.

On the stifling, humid morning of August 4, 1892, somebody used an ax or hatchet to hack to death Lizzie's stepmother and, an hour later, her father. Lizzie was soon arrested, held in jail for nearly a year, then put on trial for thirteen days.

By that time, Lizzie Borden's name had become commonplace in most of the nation's households. The items of evidence against her—and the mitigating arguments—were on the tongues of a fascinated nation. Poems praised and defended her. Songs and ditties damned her. Reporters from forty newspapers attended her trial, every day feeding a hungry population with new information and speculation.

The press's energies were well spent. Although nearly a century has served to dim the freshness of the news accounts, the information that they conveyed has helped fuel an active industry in Bordenalia. Lizzie Borden the legend now lives as Lizzie the woman never did, her reputation burnished by works of theater, scholarly treatises, university courses, and frequent retellings of the murders and the trial in books and magazine articles.

If the killings in Fall River were not perfect crimes, they proved perfectly popular. Set against the enormity of the acts was the ordinariness of the accused and her family. No scandal attached to Lizzie Borden or her parents. There was no love interest. For motive, the best that the police could fashion was frustration and rage brought about by Lizzie's prim and proper upbringing by a stern older father, whose opinions and desires—not unlike those of many heads of family of that era—dictated life in the household.

There were other suspects: Lizzie's forty-one-year-old sister, Emma; the family's maid, Bridget Sullivan; and Lizzie's uncle, John Vinnicum Morse. Each could have had a reason as strong as any imputed to Lizzie. What put Lizzie on trial was her story—or stories. She gave police contradictory accounts of events on the day of the murder. In one, she claimed to have stepped outside to the barn, just long enough for someone to enter

His head cleaved by repeated blows from an ax, Lizzie Borden's father was photographed by police on the couch where he was killed *(top)*. Lizzie herself *(above)* was captured on film shortly before her parents' murder.

and kill her father. Yet the house remained firmly locked. Lizzie admitted to ill feelings toward her stepmother. She did not explain why, earlier that fatal summer, she inquired at the pharmacy about buying prussic acid, which contains lethal portions of cyanide. Soon after that inquiry, members of her family suffered severe stomach troubles. She burned a dress, which police immediately claimed was stained with blood. Lizzie said it was paint. On the night before the murders, she confided in her best friend, "I feel depressed. I feel as if something was hanging over me that I cannot throw off," she said. "I am afraid somebody will do something."

To Lizzie Borden's defense leaped scores of women's rights groups, church members of all persuasions (Lizzie taught Sunday school), and Fall River's middle- and upper-class citizens, most of whom believed that "she couldn't have done such a thing." For its part, the government failed to produce a murder weapon or anything else to link Lizzie directly to the crime. The jury voted to acquit on the first ballot.

After her sensational trial, Lizzie Borden—later known on occasion as Miss 'Lizbeth or Miss Mary Smith Borden—went back to a quiet life of modest affluence in the gray frame house on Second Street. She lived in Fall River, largely unnoted, until her death following surgery at age sixty-seven in 1927. She lies next to her father, mother, and stepmother in the family cemetery plot.

But her case lived on, a predictable favorite of crime writers, who have never ceased retrying her and putting the other suspects in the dock. Choreographer Agnes DeMille produced a 1948 ballet, *Fall River Legend*, in which Lizzie Borden is guilty by reason of the "utter boredom" of her life. The ballet remains popular more than forty years after its first production. In 1965, composer Jack Beeson and librettist Kenward Elmslie composed an opera, *Lizzie Borden: A Family Tragedy in Three Acts.* And in 1980, Sharon Pollock wrote a play, *Blood Relations*, in which Lizzie kills for her parents' money. In all three productions, Lizzie Borden is found guilty and dies.

About 100 miles from Fall River, at the University of Massachusetts in Amherst, the Borden family ordeal was studied in detail by history students in the 1970s. The case, says professor Stephen Nissenbaum, reveals "tensions generated by social mobility and industrialization in nineteenth century America." Nissenbaum, like many twentieth-century analysts, feels that Lizzie was acquitted by a jury of her peers because upper-middle class Fall River could not face the possibility of such dark doings by its children against their parents.

New England's millworkers had no such reservations. Not long after the Borden murders, from the streets of Fall River and other cities rose a ditty that has endured like no other bit of Bordenalia: *Lizzie Borden took an ax/ And gave her mother forty whacks;/ When she saw what she had done/ She gave her father forty-one.*

The city of Fall River locked Lizzie and the Borden murders in an official closet for many years. But the Fall River Historical Society—whose museum, crammed with Borden memorabilia, sells Lizzie paperweights—scheduled an elaborate centennial observation for 1992, featuring scholarly symposia, performances of Lizzie plays and DeMille's ballet—and a reenactment of the trial of Fall River's most famous citizen. □

Memorializing the Borden murders, the American Ballet Theater danced Agnes DeMille's ballet *Fall River Legend* in New York in June of 1990.

Jack in the Jugular

As dank and shadowy as a London fog, but far more enduring, mystery still swirls about the gruesome murders committed in 1888 by the psychopath known as Jack the Ripper. Not only mystery, but a kind of public mania: Although the Ripper claimed just five victims in a ten-week spree (all prostitutes who lived anonymously in the grimy, gin-steeped London slum district of Whitechapel), the killings attracted the morbidly curious of the time—and have held the attention of every generation since.

The known facts of the case are few and simple. Early on the morning of August 31, forty-two-year-old Mary Ann Nichols was discovered lying in a street, her skirt pushed up, her throat slashed so violently that her head was al-

most severed, and her stomach hacked open. She was the first victim. A week later, the killer visited his perverted appetites on forty-seven-year-old Annie Chapman. In one night, September 30, forty-four-year-old Elizabeth Stride and forty-three-year-old Catherine Eddowes were killed. All the women had had their throats cut and their viscera torn out. Then there was a hiatus from horror until November 9, when, working for two hours in the privacy of the room of twenty-four-year-old Mary Kelly, the killer performed his most elabo-

rate mutilation yet, leaving body parts scattered around the disemboweled corpse.

After the first murders, word of the horrors swept through London and scores of police descended on Whitechapel to patrol the streets. Tradesmen formed a vigilance committee to keep watch in the night. It was all in vain.

Thousands of letters were sent to the police, some expressing apprehension, some claiming to identify the killer, others venting every sort of hate and rage.

Cards representing witnesses, police, and suspects are among the pieces of a Jack the Ripper board game published in 1983.

On October 1, a London news organization received a letter purporting to be from the murderer. "I keep on hearing the police have caught me but they wont fix me just yet," the missive said. "My knife's nice and sharp I want to get to work right away if I get a chance. Good luck. yours truly Jack the Ripper."

The name stuck, although the police were inclined to regard the letter as a hoax. They were less certain about a package sent to the Whitechapel vigilance committee about two weeks later: It contained half a human kidney. The sender said he had fried and eaten the other half.

The killings ended with the mutilation of Mary Kelly. Why they stopped will probably never be known. The police theorized that the killer had committed suicide: Their chief suspect was an unstable and sexually disturbed barrister, one Montague J. Druitt, who drowned himself in the Thames on New Year's Eve. But there were many other theories about Jack's identity. Some thought he was a man by the name of Oscar Kosminski, who was locked away in an asylum for the criminally insane in 1889, or a Russian doctor, Michael Ostrog, who had been committed to insane asylums several times. Other suspects included Alexander Pedachenko, a czarist secret agent in London at the time, and Queen Victoria's deranged grandson, the duke of Clarence. The possibility was even raised that the murderer was a woman, perhaps an abortionist known to Whitechapel's prostitutes. Latter-day Ripperologists, as they call themselves, have identified nearly 200 "suspects."

Fascination with the crimes has yielded more than 250 books; countless magazine articles; fifty plays, movies, and television programs; and one musical comedy. Computer games and board games have been devised for would-be sleuths. A London pub took its name from Jack the Ripper, and London tour guides happily—and profitably—conduct sightseers to the Whitechapel murder scenes. □

Odd Man Out

Although the finger of guilt appeared to point her way, Adelaide Bartlett (below) was acquitted of murdering her husband in 1886. Her defense was aided as much by the peculiarities of the victim as by the brilliance of her attorney.

From the start, the Bartletts had an unusual marriage. Adelaide was evidently the illegitimate child of a Frenchwoman and a rich Englishman whose identity would never be revealed. When Adelaide reached the age of nineteen, the father arranged that she marry a thirty-year-old London grocer named Edwin Bartlett. A substantial dowry enabled Edwin to expand his business. It seemed, indeed, that business was all Edwin cared about. Soon after their wedding, he sent Adelaide away to school for three years to improve her education.

When she returned, the couple's conjugal situation was, at best, troubled, although the facts would never be clear. The only certainty is that a young Methodist minister, the Reverend George Dyson, entered into the picture and began spending a great deal of time in the Bartlett household, often alone with Adelaide, with the curtains drawn. The husband seemed to encourage the relationship, especially after his health entered a steep decline. His mind, too, began to slip: Edwin believed he was under a hypnotic spell; he imagined worms were eating his insides; he wept profusely, claiming it was because he was happy; and he could only go to sleep if his wife was holding his big toe.

Adelaide Bartlett asked Dyson to buy her some chloroform. She would ◊

13

use it to help her husband sleep, she told the minister. On January 1, 1886—having, she claimed, provided no more sleep assistance during the night than toe holding—she woke to find her husband dead. It was subsequently determined that he had died from the ingestion of chloroform.

The forensic evidence was mystifying. A large amount of the liquid chloroform was found in Edwin Bartlett's stomach, but there was no evidence of inflammation of the mouth or throat, which should have resulted from swallowing the volatile poison. Murkier still was the nature of the relationship between husband and wife. The defense attorney—a star of British jurisprudence, apparently hired by Adelaide's father—argued that Edwin was dying, wanted his wife to find happiness with Dyson, and committed suicide by gulping the poison and subsiding into a peaceful sleep. The jury was not sure this was what had occurred, but it could not find a clear answer to the puzzle. Adelaide Bartlett went free, even though the verdict admitted to the "gravest suspicion" of her involvement. The jurors were not alone. One of the most prominent men of British medicine was subsequently heard to say, "Now that she's acquitted, she should tell us, in the interests of science, how she did it." □

Remembrance of Things Past

Remorse—in his case for a double murder committed in Paris in 1879—was not a feeling that Arnold Walder *(below)* comprehended. Gloating triumph, on the other hand, was an emotion Walder savored to the last drop.

Little is known of Walder's origins. Evidently he worked as a barber, a bellhop, and a weaver before taking a job as an assistant in a Pari-

sian apothecary shop at the age of twenty-two. Chafing at the low pay, he began stealing bottles of perfume from the store and selling them at a discount. But this seemed a tedious way to acquire the sort of spending money Arnold Walder felt he needed, so he bludgeoned his employer and a female servant to death and left their bodies in the cellar. He may have presided over the pharmacy for a day, ringing up sales before pocketing the cash and fleeing.

The police soon lost his trail, depriving him of the thrill of the chase. They received an intriguing note: "I have committed suicide. Better that than the terror of the guillotine." Unbelieving, the police redoubled their efforts to find Walder, but to no avail. The note turned out to be a forgery, but the correspondence that would follow it was entirely real. In his own perverse way, the young Walder had committed a perfect crime. Lest the achievement be forgotten, he wrote to the Paris police every year thereafter on the anniversary of the murders, for twenty-five years sending them a note pointing out that he was still at large. He was never caught. □

No Way Out

Susan Winslow, proprietress of a house of prostitution in Chicago in the 1890s, had a built-in defense against attempts to take her into police custody: At 450 pounds, the madam was too big to remove from her premises. Winslow's width exceeded the size of any window or door of her miserable shack; police could not figure out how she had entered it in the first place.

Finally, after a long stream of complaints about her operation and the issuance of scores of warrants for her arrest, officers broke the case by breaking up her place of business.

First, they removed the back door from its hinges. Next, they sawed out the frame and about two feet of the wall. Then long planks were inserted to serve as skids. Finally, a rope was looped around Winslow's bounteous waist, and a horse dragged her out. It was in every respect a brilliant extraction, except for the splinters that the madam bitterly complained about all the way to the police station. □

Man with the Golden Leg

Like many a man placed in proximity to gold, Orville Harington surrendered to greed. The temptation was undeniably acute. At that pivotal moment in 1919, he saw himself as an almost miraculous combination of the right person in the right place: the right person because he had a perfect way of pilfering the gold without detection; and the right place because he was employed at the Denver Mint and was thus surrounded by bullion.

His modus operandi stemmed from a disability; Harington had lost a leg in a childhood accident. He was educated as a mining engineer but had worked for years as a low-level employee in the mint's refinery. Bitterness brewed over this gap between potential and reality. It bubbled over when Harington realized that his leg's prosthetic replacement, a hollow wooden limb, was a perfect carrier for a three-pound gold ingot.

Once the idea had dawned on him, he proved a fearful drain on the national treasury, smuggling out bars of gold night after night, until ninety of them were hidden in his basement. Officials at the mint were aware of the losses, but they had no suspect—until one of Harington's fellow workers surprised Harington with an ingot in his hand. Looking guilty, Harington shoved it back into a nearby stack.

The event proved to be his undoing. A Secret Service agent was assigned to surreptitiously monitor the suspect's activities. One day, a gold bar was placed near Harington's workbench. By the end of the shift, it was gone—and so was Harington's career as a thief. Taken into custody, the man with the golden leg confessed to his long smuggling campaign. His plan, he said, was to stop stealing after a while, work for another year at the mint to deflect any suspicion, then buy an abandoned mine, where his takings—melted and sprinkled in the tunnels—would enable him to safely strike it rich. □

The window in Orville Harington's artificial leg allowed him to pilfer ingots from Denver's mint.

A .45-Caliber Trump

The 1920 murder of Joseph Elwell (*below*) was a tabloid writer's dream—a yeasty mix of wealth, fame, socialites, and sex. To add to its headline-generating merits, the case offered investigators a mind-teasing puzzle and a profusion of suspects. The only trouble was the story had no ending.

Elwell was an unusual man. Although he worked briefly as a hardware salesman in Brooklyn, his true calling was cards, especially bridge—a game in which he was well-served by a phenomenal memory. Leaving hardware behind, Elwell began to win large sums of money at gambling clubs frequented by tony New Yorkers. He added to his income by teaching bridge to society women and publishing two best-selling books about the game, *Elwell on Bridge* and *Elwell's Advanced Bridge*. At the time of his death at the age of forty-four, the cardplayer owned a yacht, a substantial art collection, a stable of racehorses in Kentucky, and four houses.

The end of the dizzying climb came at his three-story Manhattan town house, an opulent residence that included a special top-floor boudoir where he entertained an endless succession of females—showgirls, matronly bridge pupils, their daughters, anyone of the opposite sex who seemed a candidate for seduction. To ensure that the chamber never lacked visitors, he maintained a card index of the telephone numbers and affectionate nicknames of fifty-three favorite female friends, many from New York's loftier social circles, and a goodly number of them married.

This file (a "love index," newspapers called it) became of great interest to police after the lion of the boudoir and bridge table was found sitting in his living room on the morning of June 11 with a bullet hole between his eyes. Detectives quickly determined that Elwell had been out on the town the night before with a fashionable female friend but had quarreled with her and returned home alone. An inveterate night owl, Elwell had stayed up, placing telephone calls and prowling about the house in his red pajamas. Milk bottles were left on his doorstep at 6:00 a.m. When the postman brought the mail at 7:20, the milk bottles were gone. The housekeeper discovered Elwell less than an hour later, breathing his last. He had been shot as he opened the mail; one blood-stained letter was in his lap, and others were scattered on the floor in front of him. There was no sign of a struggle, and nothing had been stolen.

The housekeeper had not recognized Elwell at first. She knew her employer as a handsome man with thick hair and a dazzling smile. The victim slumped in the living-room chair was bald and almost toothless. Police would later find dentures in his bedroom and forty expensive toupees in a closet. Their first thought was that a woman had done it, and they proceeded to question all fifty-three of the entries in the card index, destroying several marriages in the process. But doubts began to grow. The murder weapon was a .45-caliber pistol—a heavy weapon for a woman to use. And it seemed odd that the vain Elwell would play host to a female visitor without his hair or teeth in place. When the love index yielded up nothing but solid alibis, newspapers speculated about other possible killers—vengeful fathers, jealous husbands, gambling victims, rivals in the horse world.

But after a while, even this sort of journalistic stoking could not keep the story hot. Elwell faded from the front pages, sinking to a lower but more enduring level of fame as an authority on the intricacies of bridge whose sordid demise was never explained. □

A Sanguinary Yule

For the little West Texas town of Cisco, Christmas in 1927 lacked its usual cheer. The problem was Santa Claus—and also Santa's helpers. On December 23, an ex-convict in a Santa suit, aided by three friends, descended on the First National Bank in Cisco with larcenous intent. What followed was a blend of violence and ineptitude that would ultimately put St. Nick's neck in a noose.

The ringleader of the heist, a former Cisco resident named Marshall Ratliff, had dressed up as Santa for the sensible purpose of avoiding recognition. His assistants were out-of-towners and did not bother with disguises; they arrived in a stolen Buick, parked the car in an alley nearby, and strolled into the bank behind their white-bearded leader. Then the four drew guns and ordered the people in the bank to raise their hands. A six-year-old girl, understandably confused, screamed, "They're shooting Santa Claus!" Her mother dragged her out a side door and ran for the police.

Reversing his usual Yuletide role, Santa pulled a bag from beneath his red suit and filled it with $162,000 in cash and securities. But by then police officers were

rushing to the scene, backed by a small army of gun-toting townsfolk who wanted in on the action—at least partly because the Texas State Bankers Association had made a standing offer of a $5,000 bounty for any dead bank robber. Seeing their peril, the four men grabbed a number of hostages, including two young girls, and headed for their getaway vehicle. But any hope that the citizenry would hold their fire out of fear for the hostages' safety was soon disabused. Pistols, rifles, and shotguns blazed from every corner and doorway, and the robbers replied with a fusillade of defensive fire. Within seconds, one of Santa's helpers was grievously wounded; two police officers were mortally struck; and several hostages were shot, although not seriously hurt. In all, more than 250 shots were fired, resulting in eleven casualties.

But the mayhem was far from over. The robbers forced the two children into the car and roared out of the alley, the Buick yawing as air leaked from a bullet-punctured tire. At the edge of town, the men slued to a stop and, brandishing guns, commandeered an Oldsmobile driven by a fourteen-year-old lad. After transferring everything into this car, they prepared to resume their flight, only to discover that the wise young driv- ◊

Grim-faced lawmen and curious citizens *(top)* flank two of Cisco's bungling bank robbers *(tieless in right center)*, who survived the gunfire that was partly motivated by the poster at right.

$5,000 REWARD
For DEAD Bank Robbers
$5,000 cash will be paid for each Bank Robber legally killed while Robbing this bank

er had pocketed the keys before disappearing. Pursuers were now close; a shot hit another of the robbers in the arm. He remained in action, but one of the gang was dying. Leaving the fatally wounded man in the Olds, the three remaining bandits leaped back in the Buick with their hostages and thumped away on the now-flat tire. After a few minutes, they realized that they had forgotten their loot. It was back in the Olds.

But that was the least of their problems. An armada of cars was close behind. The robbers led it down dirt roads and into an area of thick brush about four miles from town. There, they released the two girls and made good their escape—temporarily. Later that day, lawmen from eight counties joined the hunt. The three outlaws managed to stay ahead of the pursuers, then circled back to Cisco and stole another car. But in their haste to escape, the robbers drove this vehicle into a cattle guard and wrecked it. Still, auto theft was one of their few proven skills: The crooks went through two more cars before they were finally run to earth. By then, Ratliff had six bullet wounds and one of his companions had seven. The other was miraculously unscathed.

Justice took several courses. One of the gang received a sentence of ninety-nine years; another went to the electric chair; Ratliff was sentenced to death, as well, but the erstwhile Santa bought time by trying on a new disguise. A recent court decision stated that a prisoner could not be executed if judged insane. On death row, Ratliff began to talk deliriously, refuse his food, and lie in a catatonic trance for hours at a time.

It proved a lethally shallow trance. One day, an elderly guard left the apparently harmless prisoner's cell door open. Ratliff slipped out, found a gun, and shot the guard before being subdued.

At once, Ratliff relapsed into his trance, but the local citizenry had now had enough. As the life of the wounded guard ebbed away, a mob stormed the jail, seized Ratliff, looped a rope about his neck, and strung him up.

A grand jury refused to indict any members of the lynch mob. □

A Spanish thief of middle age proved to be just too long in the tooth for his physically demanding line of work. The fifty-six-year-old robber tripped and swallowed his own false teeth after grabbing 18,000 pesetas ($170) from a woman in Alicante. He choked to death when the dentures became stuck in his windpipe.

A Laggard Verdict

Although truth and justice are supposed to be inseparable, sometimes only one is served. Persuasive theory indicates that justice never caught up with the man who murdered Julia Wallace in Liverpool in 1931, but his guilt would become clear in the end.

The victim was the wife of

William Herbert Wallace, a mild-mannered agent of the Prudential Insurance Company whose life was a model of quiet propriety. The day before the murder, William Wallace was handed an innocuous-seeming telephone message: A man named R. M. Qualtrough had called and given an address, asking Wal-

William and Julia Wallace posed for these family photographs before he was framed for murdering her.

lace to come by on the following evening to discuss an insurance policy for Qualtrough's daughter. At the appointed time, Wallace searched for the house, finally concluding neither it nor Qualtrough existed. He returned home to a nightmare. His wife lay on the parlor floor, her head smashed in by a heavy object. Evidently, money had been taken from a box in which Wallace kept cash receipts.

When the police arrived, they concluded that the victim had known her killer, since there was no sign of forced entry. Soon police attention focused on Wallace himself, whose air of almost fussy calm seemed peculiar to them. He was placed under arrest.

At the request of the police, Wallace provided the names of several people who might have been readily admitted to the house by his wife. One—the likeliest suspect, in his judgment—was twenty-two-year-old former Prudential employee Richard Gordon Parry, who knew the house well, knew about the cash box, and had been fired at Wallace's instigation for mishandling accounts. The police questioned Parry briefly. He said he had been with his fiancée at the time of the killing; she verified this.

Wallace was charged with his wife's murder. At the trial, the defendant's emotionless demeanor worked against him. The jury chose to ignore the testimony of defense witnesses that Julia Wallace was alive at the time her husband was searching for the bogus address. Persuaded that the murder had been committed earlier and that the mysterious caller had been invented by Wallace to create an alibi, the jurors pronounced him guilty. He was sentenced to death.

The evidence was so equivocal, however, that the Court of Criminal Appeal overturned the jury's verdict—the first such reversal since the establishment of the court in 1907. Wallace went free, but local prejudice forced him to move from Liverpool, and he died of kidney failure in 1933.

Many decades later, a British crime writer, Jonathan Goodman, looked into the case, concentrating on the man Wallace had pointed to, Richard Gordon Parry. Goodman determined that, in 1931, Parry had possessed a considerable criminal record, which the police had unaccountably failed to discover. Parry's then fiancée was located; she acknowledged that the alibi Parry gave was untrue. He had not been with her. (She had also admitted the lie to Wallace's lawyer shortly after Wallace's death, but the lawyer had not bothered to inform the police.)

In 1981, a half-century after the murder, Goodman announced in a radio broadcast that William Wallace had been right all along: Parry—by then deceased—had killed Julia Wallace. □

Murder and Magic

In the series of murders he masterminded in the little Swedish town of Sala between 1930 and 1936, Sigvard Thurneman (right) aspired to perfection—but that was more from a sense of order than from any great fear of being caught. He saw himself as a sort of priestly interpreter of a higher law, although in the end it was simple human law that halted his grisly antics.

Sickly, feral in appearance, and a loner from early childhood, Thurneman became deeply interested in ritual magic as a teenager. He founded ◊

a local branch of a secret society known as the Magic Circle, drawing other susceptible youths into its embrace. The key idea of the Magic Circle, as formulated by Sigvard Thurneman, was the absence of good and evil in the world: Stealing property or taking a life were merely changes in the condition of things, of no moral significance. A bylaw of the Sala branch stated that the group had the unrestricted right to "wipe out" any member who was disobedient, undependable, or too talkative.

Wiping out others—all outside the circle, so far as is known—became a favorite activity for Thurneman. In 1930, he shot a taxi driver in the head to prove to himself that he was properly free of feeling for a victim. In 1933, he enlisted two helpers for a more ambitious extermination. Dressing up as a pair of policemen with a prisoner in tow, the trio talked their way into the house of a man who was known to have a large amount of cash on hand. At midnight—a time chosen for ritualistic reasons—they shot the homeowner and his housekeeper, took the money, and set the house aflame in order to conceal their deed. That tactic notwithstanding, the police registered the incident as murder, but the case remained temporarily unsolved.

The following year, the Sala occultists targeted an elderly woman, an eccentric who carried around bags thought to contain money. Hitching a hose to the exhaust pipe of a car, they pumped carbon monoxide gas into her house—again at midnight. When they entered, she was still alive. The bags proved to hold bits of rubbish. As before, they set fire to the house,

incinerating its dazed occupant.

In 1936, Thurneman and two partners stole a car in Stockholm, drove back to Sala, and waylaid a bicyclist who was carrying the payroll of a local quarrying operation. They shot him down, grabbed the money, and raced away, certain that they would never be linked to the murder. But a few days later, a farmworker walked into the town's police station and identified one of the killers, Erike Nedstrom: The workman was quite sure, since Nedstrom had asked him to take part in the act.

Nedstrom, in turn, identified his partners in murder. The Magic-Circle members talked freely about their exploits, enough to send the accomplices to prison for life. Thurneman, judged criminally insane, spent thirty-two years in mental institutions. Released in 1969, he moved to a Stockholm suburb, where he lived quietly until his death ten years later—having possibly concluded that conventional morality was worth observing after all. □

Bad Chemistry

John George Haigh thought he knew how to get away with murder—and he put his theory to the test at least six times between 1944 and 1949. His calculations, however, proved to be fatally flawed, and in the end, Haigh paid for his victims' lives with his own.

In retrospect, it seems clear that upbringing had something to do with Haigh's outlook and tastes. Born in 1909 and raised in a Yorkshire village, he was the only child of parents who belonged to a stern religious sect that stressed constant prayer and an avoidance of any frivolity. The father told the boy that his mother was an angel—literally—and the couple built a high wall around the house to barricade it against evil spirits. In the face of such eccentricity, young Haigh showed no signs of rebellion; he did well in school, became a choirboy, and appeared eager to please. But as an adult,

A policeman leads handcuffed John Haigh to his 1949 trial in London for the murder and disposal by acid of Olive Durand-Deacon (far right).

he drifted into a variety of swindling schemes, theft, and ultimately a unique approach to murder.

The climactic crime of his life took shape in a small London hotel where Haigh lived in 1949. There he struck up a friendship with another resident, Olive Durand-Deacon, a well-to-do, sixty-nine-year-old widow. When the dapper, always-polite Haigh told her that he was an engineer and developer of inventions, she confessed that she had an invention of her own—a design for artificial fingernails that she thought might be made out of plastic.

At that point in his life, Haigh was broke and bouncing checks in all directions. Nonetheless, he had acquired the use of a small warehouse south of London, a ramshackle place he called his factory. He invited Durand-Deacon to visit it with him, with an eye to future fingernail manufacturing. She agreed to come—and told a friend about the planned trip.

At the factory, Haigh wasted no time in going about his real business. He shot Durand-Deacon in the back of the head and removed her expensive Persian-lamb coat and her jewelry, later to be pawned. Next, he dumped her body in a forty-five-gallon drum and filled it with sulfuric acid. Then, tired by his exertions, Haigh went to a nearby restaurant for tea and a poached egg on toast.

The next day, apparently trying to establish his own innocence, Haigh went to Durand-Deacon's friend and inquired about the missing woman. He said she had made an appointment to meet him and had never showed up. The friend insisted on going to the police, and Haigh joined her, repeating his story. He then drove to his warehouse and inspected the barrel. Some fat and a piece of bone were floating on the surface; he added more acid to hasten the reaction. A day later, he returned, concluded that Durand-Deacon was now nonexistent, and poured the sludgy acid onto the ground outside.

But the police were on his trail. Scotland Yard had discovered that Haigh had a criminal record, and soon they learned about his warehouse. Investigators hastened to the scene and found his gun, a cleaner's receipt for the Persian-lamb coat, and various equipment used for handling acid. When they confronted Haigh with these facts, he pulled what he considered to be his trump card. "I've destroyed her with acid," he boldly admitted. "Every trace has gone. How can you prove murder if there's no body?" Then, almost boastfully, he told them that he had killed a young man and his parents five years earlier and another couple the previous year—in all cases for money, and each time following the murder with his standard evidence-destroying chemistry. He had also drunk his victims' blood, he said—a claim that was never verified and that may have been meant as part of an insanity defense.

Haigh uttered these revelations because he believed—incorrectly—that British law prevented prosecution for homicide unless a body could be found.

Besides his faulty legal logic, there was something else wrong with Haigh's plan: The acid had not completed its work on Durand-Deacon. When experts examined the sludge Haigh had poured from the barrel, they found twenty-eight pounds of fat, some gallstones, part of a foot, eighteen bone fragments, a set of dentures, and several other telltale remnants.

A few months later, Haigh was tried for murder. The jury took seventeen minutes to reach its verdict: He was guilty, and he would hang. □

A New York City detective dusts for fingerprints around the hole quick-working thieves battered through Tiffany's window in robbing the upscale emporium of more than $160,000 in jewels.

Tiffany's Before Breakfast

Tiffany and Company, New York's elegant Fifth Avenue jewelry store, rose from humble beginnings in 1837 to modern prominence by quietly flouting the conventions of its competitors. While catering to the rich and famous—Tiffany's once furnished a bicycle studded with diamonds and rubies to actress Sarah Bernhardt—the store also manufactured guns, surgical instruments, and airplane parts during three wars. And, although other jewelers removed window displays on weekends or substituted inexpensive stand-ins, Tiffany's displayed the most elegant items at all times, so that strollers could savor the tasteful magnificence at any time—and perhaps return to buy during business hours.

The tradition made Tiffany's windows at Fifth Avenue and Fifty-seventh Street favorites of window-shoppers great and small, memorialized in 1958 by author Truman Capote in the short novel *Breakfast at Tiffany's.* The book's heroine, a young woman improbably named Holly Golightly, periodically lifts her sagging spirits by visiting the store in the early morning hours to gaze dreamily at the glittering gems.

But in the gray light of dawn on Sunday, August 10, 1958, thieves shattered tradition by boldly bludgeoning their way through two large display windows on Fifth Avenue and making off with four diamond-encrusted items valued at more than $160,000. The break-in was accomplished within a period of twenty minutes, as two store guards tended to other duties inside. The heist was discovered at 6:15 a.m. by New York City patrolman Thomas Connolly, whose beat covered a four-and-a-half-block stretch of Fifth Avenue between Fifty-second and Fifty-seventh streets. Ten minutes earlier, Connolly had replaced patrolman Stanley Gibbs, who was reassigned to beef up security for the arrival of Soviet Foreign Minister Andrei Gromyko at the Waldorf-Astoria Hotel. Gibbs left his beat at 5:45.

Within minutes of Gibbs's departure for the Waldorf, the thieves struck Tiffany's, battering the huge windows with sledgehammers. Unlike normal plate-glass windows, these were constructed of two thick sheets of glass sandwiching a resilient plastic filler. The burglars' blows could not shatter it; instead, they pounded two holes about five inches in diameter. Because of their thickness, the windows were considered impregnable and were not protected by an alarm. The windows' plastic filler, intended to absorb blows that would break other panes, also absorbed the sound. That, and the display's heavy, opulent decorations, assured that the store security guards heard nothing, although they were within 150 feet of the windows at all times.

With the holes opened, the burglars deftly reached in and removed a necklace containing sixty-eight diamonds weighing a total of 50.29 carats and valued at $68,750, a second necklace containing 266 diamonds weighing 40.54 carats worth $60,000, a platinum ring featuring a 5.45-carat solitaire diamond worth $18,700, and a pin clip decorated with 164 diamonds worth $15,850. The discriminating robbers left behind two diamond-and-sapphire brooches whose total value was a mere $8,000 to $9,000.

The efficiency and timing of the theft cast suspicion on both of the security guards and on the police. But no charges were ever filed; the jewels, worth about $60,000 on the illegal market, were never recovered, and today Tiffany and Company locks up its most elegant merchandise at night. □

Moving Target

From a thief's point of view, Rembrandt van Rijn's seventeenth-century portrait of Dutch burgher Jacob de Gheyn *(above)* has many attractions. It is small—twelve inches by ten inches. It is worth about five million dollars. And it hangs—periodically at least—in south London's Dulwich Picture Gallery. On four occasions, the little masterwork has been stolen and then recovered, a record suggesting that even though it has not yet figured in a perfect crime, it is the perfect target.

The portrait first disappeared from the museum when burglars broke in one night in 1967 and took eight paintings—at the time, the biggest art theft ever. Police, acting on a telephone tip, recovered the entire haul a week later. In 1973, a visitor slipped the little gem under his coat and made for the door, only to be intercepted by guards; he wanted to make a copy, he said. In 1981, the portrait was successfully purloined but subsequently found in a London taxicab, along with three men—one a German art dealer—who were trying to fence it. After that, the museum bolted their too-tempting Rembrandt to the wall and bought a £20,000 security system. But in 1983, thieves broke through a skylight and pried the Rembrandt off with a crowbar. An anonymous tip later led to the painting's discovery in the unclaimed-luggage office of a West German train station.

The work has not strayed from its rightful premises since, but officials continue to mull over better security arrangements, including, as one has said, "building a great wall around the museum as a defense." □

Canceled Charges

Bending the finger of blame toward someone else is a time-honored defensive strategy, but rarely has it worked more neatly than in a murder trial that mesmerized Italy in the mid-1960s.

The basic ingredients of the case were not complex. On January 20, 1964, a wealthy twenty-seven-year-old Egyptian businessman named Farouk Chourbagi was found dead in his office off the fashionable Via Veneto in Rome. He had been shot repeatedly, and his face burned with acid. ◊

Appearing distraught, fur-clad Claire Ghobrial, Youssef Bebawi's former wife, waits in a Rome courtroom to testify in the couple's trial for the murder of her lover, Farouk Chourbagi.

Commando Caper

For sheer swashbuckling verve, few bank robbers have ever equaled Frenchman Albert Spaggiari, a one-time paratrooper who pulled off a brilliantly conceived heist in the city of Nice in 1976. He escaped the clutches of justice by a daredevil maneuver and assiduously kept himself in the public eye—but free—for years thereafter.

Born in 1932, Spaggiari early on displayed a cavalier attitude toward the law, running away from home at the age of seventeen with the intention of joining a gang of bandits in Sicily. Rebuffed by the Sicilian gunmen, Spaggiari enlisted in the French airborne forces and served in Indochina before concluding his military career by spending five years in jail for stealing from a bordello in Saigon. Thereafter, he became involved with right-wing extremist groups in Europe. In later days, he claimed that he embarked on the Nice venture to fund his political causes.

Whether that was true, the robbery was thoroughly commando-like in planning and execution. With as many as twenty-three accomplices, Spaggiari spent days in the dank sewers of Nice, a Mediterranean resort city, drilling through twenty-five feet of rock and masonry with heavy equipment to get to the vault of the Société Générale bank. Once inside, the burglars welded the vault door shut from the inside to protect their privacy. Then, taking periodic breaks to fortify themselves with the food and wine they had brought along, they devoted two days to opening more than 300 safe-deposit boxes.

Youssef Bebawi *(left)* confers with his lawyer during the trial in which he and his former wife accused each other of murdering her lover.

Suspicion soon fixed on two other Middle Eastern expatriates, cotton dealer Youssef Bebawi and his beautiful ex-wife, Claire Ghobrial, who had been having an affair with Chourbagi. Police determined that Bebawi and Ghobrial had registered in a hotel near Chourbagi's office just before the murder and had checked out the same day and traveled to Athens.

Both were indicted for the crime, which appeared to be some sort of bloody settling of an issue of love and honor. But as their trial unfolded, each defendant asserted innocence and accused the other of the deed. Claire insisted that Youssef had burst in on her and Chourbagi and had slaughtered her lover in a rage as she huddled in a bathroom. Youssef claimed that Claire had gone to Chourbagi's office to break off the affair and had returned crying, "I've killed him! I've killed him!"

The trial, featuring an endless stream of character witnesses but little hard evidence, provided titillating fare for Italian newspapers for almost a year and a half. In the end, the jury decided the case on the basis of an ancient and honored principle of Italian jurisprudence, *in dubio pro reo*—when in doubt, free the defendant. Youssef Bebawi and Claire Ghobrial knew which one of them was guilty; but by their perfectly offsetting accusations, they ensured that both of them would go free. □

The harvest amounted to about $10 million in money, jewels, and other valuables. One box yielded a set of pornographic pictures, possibly intended for blackmail purposes; the thieves pasted these on the walls. As they retraced their steps out of the bank on July 19, Spaggiari and his fellows left a note that read, "Without hatred, without arms, without violence."

Four months later, Spaggiari was arrested, along with other members of the gang. But little of the loot was recovered. To the surprise and relief of his warders, the tough former paratrooper proved a model prisoner—so well-behaved and co-operative that the police did not bother to guard him closely. This was, of course, as he planned it. One day while being examined by a judge, the ex-soldier went to the window of the magistrate's second-floor chamber, complaining of the heat. He opened the window, leaped out, landed expertly on the roof of a parked car, rolled off, sprang onto the passenger seat of a waiting motorcycle, and roared away to freedom. A thousand police hunted him in the area, but Spaggiari would never be caught.

Still, he did not exactly lie low. He was seen throughout Europe, gave interviews to magazines, appeared on television, and even wrote a book about the Nice robbery. Journalists said that there was no great difficulty in contacting him, if one knew how. The police did not know how.

Spaggiari died of lung cancer in 1989. His body, clad in military fatigues, was left on his mother's doorstep by unknown parties. □

Robbing Blind

If a sighted person can rob a bank, Robert Toye figured, a blind person can do it too. Afflicted with retinitis pigmentosa, an incurable, degenerative eye disease, Toye had only the dimmest vestige of vision. Nevertheless, he deftly navigated his way through seventeen bank jobs in various American cities between 1974 and 1983, biding his time in the nightspots of Las Vegas between heists.

But then, Toye always was a self-reliant sort. As a sixteen-year-old school dropout living in a park in California, he researched the tricks of mail fraud by sending away for a Postal Service manual on the topic. His first mail scam was to advertise an envelope-stuffing business—a nonexistent enterprise that could be joined by sending in a five-dollar application fee. Many more such ploys followed—until his activities landed him in federal prison in 1973. There, Toye set his sights on a new opportunity when he learned from fellow inmates that, for reasons of safety, the tellers of federally insured banks are instructed to turn over money to robbers without protest. While still in the slammer, he prepared a calling card—a one-eyed jack ◊

Burly, tattooed "Blind Bob" Toye greets visitors at Lompoc federal prison in California.

bearing the message, "Be quick, be quiet or you're dead. Put all the cash in the bag. I have a gun."

Upon his release in 1974, Toye hailed a cab and headed for the nearest target. "I told the cabdriver I had to go by the bank to pick up some money," he later recalled. He "withdrew" $8,000.

Toye's eyesight was rapidly deteriorating, but that hardly interfered with his new career. He developed the tactic of focusing on the back of someone's shoe and following the customer to a teller's window. When Toye had the cash in hand, he would unfold his white cane and hastily tap his way to the exit. This method of retreat worked flawlessly for more than half a dozen jobs. But in 1977, he stumbled into armed guards who were delivering money to a New York City bank branch that he had just relieved of several thousand dollars. He was arrested and jailed.

Six years later, Toye was on the street again—the result of a bureaucratic blunder by a halfway house, which refused to accept him because he was blind. Toye shifted his residence to Las Vegas but retained a professional preference for New York, regularly commuting by plane, taking a cab to a bank branch for a heist, and immediately returning by cab to the airport for the flight home. In three months, he pulled off nine bank jobs. But now New York City police were watching for him, and when Toye deviated from his routine in order to buy a suitcase, they grabbed him as he was tapping his way along Eighth Avenue.

This time, the prison doors slammed hard: The blind bank robber received a seventeen-year sentence. But Blind Bob—as fellow prisoners affectionately call him—has exhibited his independent spirit by attempting at least one escape. On that occasion, he made it over two fences, flattening the razor wire at the top with his cane, and was moving fast—until he ran into a pine tree. □

A Nice, Round Number

At some point over the long Columbus Day weekend in October of 1977, exactly $1 million in cash—$800,000 in new $100 bills and $200,000 in used $50 bills—disappeared from the vault of the First National Bank of Chicago. It was a number too neat to believe, the result of a crime that was equally neat—so tidy that no one has ever been prosecuted for stealing the money, nor has it been recovered.

No break-in was required. For much of the weekend, the vault was kept open—although tightly guarded—to receive large deposits from businesses. The money vanished from a cart, one of many used to deliver cash to tellers and other employees during normal bank operations. On Tuesday night after the holiday weekend, a routine count revealed that the cart in question, supposed to hold four million dollars, contained only three. Still, this was the sort of discrepancy that bookkeeping errors often caused. Feeling no great alarm, auditors spent Wednesday going over their records. To their horror, they determined that the million was really missing. Then they called in the FBI.

The federal agents assumed the heist was an inside job. Some sixty employees had access to the vault over the weekend. Agents questioned everyone, examined fingerprints, and asked workers to take lie-detector tests. Two refused—one a pregnant woman who declined on the advice of her doctor, the other a man who had worked at the bank for fourteen years.

After a little more study, the agents were sure that this man was the culprit. Three times over the weekend, they discovered, he had entered the part of the vault where the stolen money had been kept. "Although he had no business in the area, none of the other employees questioned his presence because they all knew him," said one agent. By making several trips to the cart, he could have smuggled out that amount of cash in special pockets in his clothes.

The FBI urged bank officials to keep the suspect at work so that he might be lulled into compla-

cency and perhaps show the way to the money. The bank, dubious about this advice, suspended and later fired the employee. Thereafter, the man was kept under a round-the-clock watch by teams of observers.

The suspected thief continued to live quietly in the Chicago area, the subject of relentless surveillance. Either he was not the thief, or he retained the calculating coolness that enabled him to pluck precisely a million dollars from under the noses of bank guards. □

Police Story

When attempting to pull off the perfect crime, it helps to be a cop—a fact demonstrated by a mega-heist of the Depositors Trust Company bank of Medford, Massachusetts, on Memorial Day, 1980.

Of the six men involved, three were ranking policemen: Lieutenant Thomas Doherty of the Medford police and Captain Gerald Clemente and Sergeant Joseph Bangs of Boston's Metropolitan Police Department. All, it turned out, had been active in the local burglary trade for years. Their three accomplices were thugs skilled in such useful arts as safecracking and disconnecting alarms.

The Depositors Trust break-in would be the cops' biggest job yet, and they used their positions to advantage during their careful preparations. Months beforehand, the officers monitored the bank's

alarm system from the police station while one of their helpers experimented with various disconnection tactics at the scene of the planned crime. When the moment for action came, the conspirators donned gloves to eliminate the possibility of fingerprints and wore long-sleeved shirts and head-covering nylon stockings to ensure that no telltale hairs or flakes of skin were left behind.

After picking the lock of a door in an adjacent building, they broke

through a wall to reach a room above the vault, then attempted to drill through the eighteen inches of reinforced concrete separating them from the money. Doherty, in policeman's uniform, stood guard outside. During the night, the owner of an adjacent restaurant turned up to do some work; the lieutenant told him to go home, explaining that there had been a number of break-ins in the neighborhood and his light might attract hooligans. ◊

Optician Ed Burns of Medford displays the hole in his store's wall through which burglars entered the Depositors Trust Company bank next door.

Atop the vault, the others were unable to penetrate the concrete with drills, but the men had come prepared for such an eventuality: They blew a hole through the concrete with dynamite. Once inside the vault, the group rifled some 714 safe-deposit boxes, making off with an estimated $1.5 million in cash and perhaps $15 million worth of jewelry.

As soon as the heist was discovered Tuesday morning, Clemente and Doherty came under suspicion. Doherty had been seen in the neighborhood, and he and Clemente—known to be cronies—both had unsavory reputations. But they had done such a professional job of covering their tracks that the robbery could not be pinned on them. When the heat abated after a couple of years, Clemente invested his share of the take in real estate, and the professional criminals pursued their various underworld interests—although one was almost killed in a dispute over the loot.

Doherty and Bangs went into the drug business on a grand scale, and the Depositors Trust team came to grief as a result. In 1985, Bangs and Doherty quarreled over $14,000 that Doherty owed to Bangs for drugs.

Pressed for the money and feeding a ravenous cocaine habit by then, Doherty and his brother-in-law ambushed Bangs, riddling him with buckshot. Bangs managed to stumble to safety, and his attackers were arrested for attempted murder. But Bangs was now in another kind of trouble: In the trunk of his car, police found jewelry that was traced to the Depositors Trust robbery nearly five years earlier.

Identifying the course of least resistance, Bangs agreed to testify against his former colleagues in return for immunity. On the stand, he sang his heart out and sent the others away to prison for lengthy terms. He then headed westward for life in a federal-witness-protection program.

Bangs was happy with the outcome—but he might have been happier if the quarrel with Doherty had occurred just a little bit later. Six months hence, the statute of limitations would have rendered the whole gang unconvictable for the Depositors Trust caper. □

John Wojtowicz spent six years in prison for the bungled 1972 New York bank holdup that was replayed in a popular movie, *Dog Day Afternoon*. Neither holdup nor movie paid: Police killed Wojtowicz's partner during the escape, and by law, Wojtowicz was forced to turn over his $50,000 movie fee to a fund for aiding crime victims.

Four impassive Depositors Trust burglars attend their trial, from left: Thomas Doherty, Kenneth Holmes, Francis O'Leary, and Gerald Clemente.

Changeling

The Reverend John David Terry wanted a fresh start. Unhappy in his work as pastor of a Pentecostal church in Nashville, Tennessee, suffering from what he later speculated was "burn-out or middle-age crazies," he also had some concerns about his personal freedom: Terry had embezzled $33,000 from his church. So he decided to pull a disappearing act.

In the spring of 1987, he made preparations. From an old newspaper, Terry chose a name that would be his new identity: Jerry Winston Milom, who had died by drowning at the age of seven in 1951. The minister took out $150,000 in life insurance for the benefit of his family. He spent about $5,000 on a motorcycle for his future self. Then, on the night of June 15, he carried various sorts of equipment to his church—a gun, a butcher's saw and knife (he knew how to use them, having worked as a part-time butcher to make ends meet), and gasoline.

At the church was the person Terry had chosen to assume the role of his old self, handyman James Chester Matheny, who bore a physical resemblance to him. Terry shot Matheny, expertly decapitated him to prevent dental matching, cut off his right forearm and patches of flesh on his shoulders to remove identifying tattoos, splashed gasoline around the church and ignited it. Matheny/Terry having been disposed of,

Terry/Milom then purred away on his new motorcycle to throw the spare body parts in a lake.

Despite the scheme's careful construction, it failed. Firefighters arrived in time to save the church and preserve the butchered corpse. The police soon identified Matheny and launched a search for Terry. A few days later, Terry turned himself in. At his trial, he pleaded not guilty, then self-defense, then in-sanity. The jury gave him the electric chair, but the sentence was reduced to life imprisonment. This reprieve coincided with logic Terry had expressed at his sentencing. "Because of me, there's a widow," he said. "I would certainly hate for my wife to become a widow." □

Preacher John David Terry altered his appearance during his murder trial *(top left, with beard)* and after it *(below).*

A Touch Too Much of TNT

When four young locals decided to blow open a bank's night-deposit box in the Danish town of Munkebo in 1987, they chose a time that they figured would delay discovery of the robbery. The deed would be done early in the morning of Pentecost Sunday, June 7. Since Monday was a bank holiday, no one would be wise to the crime until Tuesday morning, long after they had made good their escape.

Getting in would require a deft application of dynamite—just enough to smash the bank's vault-like night-deposit box without making enough noise to alert police. Although the logic is unclear, their plan called for slipping the bomb through the bank's mail slot, allowing it to explode close to the target. Presumably, the walls of the building would muffle the sound of the explosion.

The plotters—two men and two women, all between eighteen and twenty-four—were new to safe-cracking and not exactly sure how much dynamite was needed to do the job without attracting attention, but they trusted their instincts in calibrating the charge. Their instincts came up short.

At precisely 2:55 Sunday morning, a tremendous clap of thunder shattered the sleep of every inhabitant of Munkebo. It set windows vibrating as far as five miles away. The roof of the bank lifted skyward. Furniture and equipment sailed outward in ballistic arcs. The mail slot that had admitted the dynamite hurtled through the air and embedded itself deep in the wall of a shop across the street. As the rumbling echoes died away, the would-be robbers could see that the bank was destroyed—virtually blown to pieces—as was a grocery store next door. Only one thing was left standing at the scene: the night-deposit box.

The inept burglars fled, only to be tracked down a week later. To add to their woes, they learned that the excessive use of explosives was not their only serious miscalculation. On the occasion of their aggressive assault, the night-deposit box was empty. □

In Record Crime

In his lifelong trade—armed robbery—Jack Kelm was a hard worker, and retirement held no appeal. Between 1986 and 1989, as his eightieth birthday came and went, he kept busy holding up banks, supermarkets, and other businesses. In Colorado, he collected about $25,000—to supplement his Social Security checks, he later explained.

On March 28, 1989, Kelm—then eighty-two—set his hand to yet another typical job: He walked into First Bank South of Longmont, Colorado, pulled a gun (actually a loud but harmless starter's pistol loaded with blanks—his standard weapon), seized a bag holding about $9,000 in cash, and fled on a stolen ten-speed bike. Unfortunately for the octogenarian robber, the bag was booby-trapped and began spewing a decidedly suspicious cloud of red dye. Besides, Jack Kelm just could not pedal the way he used to. A family of onlookers gave chase in their car. The car's driver jumped out and wrestled Kelm to the ground before the robber got out of the parking lot, bringing to an end one of the longest criminal careers on record.

With that, Kelm decided to retire. He confessed to a string of robberies in the previous few years. But those heists turned out to be only a tiny fraction of his lifelong output. Checking their files, police discovered that Kelm began stealing as a boy in Illinois back in the days of John Dillinger and continued at his calling all across America. Stints behind bars consumed forty years of Kelm's adult life, but he reduced these periods of enforced idleness by escaping twice from Colorado prisons and once from a Florida chain gang.

And he did his level best to make up for the lost time, committing an estimated 1,000 robberies before his old legs gave out in Longmont. □

A policeman handcuffs eighty-two-year-old armed robber Jack Kelm following his capture escaping from a bank hold-up in Longmont, Colorado.

Wedding Bust

For drug dealers in and around Flint, Michigan, in September 1990, it seemed a splendid social occasion: Fast Eddie Leno, a drug czar who had recently appeared in the area, requested the pleasure of their company at the marriage of his daughter Debbie to one of his minions, Danny Brown. No matter that the invitees did not know these people well; Leno and Brown showed every sign of being important customers, so twelve of the dealers showed up.

It seemed to be a well-run underworld wedding. Guests were asked to check their weapons at the door of the rented hall, and a quick inspection by a hand-held metal detector had a further reassuring effect. After the minister tied the knot, toasts were made, music played, and the guests danced for an hour. Fast Eddie was clearly a man of style: At each table were matchbooks bearing the names of the bride and groom and the message, "Thank you for sharing our joy." Then the band struck up the pop tune "I Fought the Law (And the Law Won)." A voice announced that everyone who was a cop should stand. More than half the guests rose. The bride pulled a snubnosed revolver from under her gown; Fast Eddie (in reality, a local police chief) drew a Walther pistol from his cummerbund; the minister produced a nine millimeter semiautomatic from the folds of his robe; members of the band (named SPOC—COPS spelled backward) displayed enough additional firepower to discourage any resistance. The pseudonymous Danny Brown, for his part, unveiled a fistful of arrest warrants.

All in all, the occasion was a great success, saving police the effort and uncertainties of hunting down the dealers individually. Understandably, the dealer-guests were resentful. As the elated cops posed with their prisoners for the benefit of news photographers, one handcuffed dealer remarked—perhaps superfluously—that he would not have come if he had known he was going to be arrested. □

The beaming "bride," Flint police officer Debra Williams, shows off her gun and garter holster after successfully snaring drug dealers at her 1990 "wedding."

Watch the Neighbors

The Neighborhood Watch program, in which citizens keep tabs on events near their homes and swap notes with the local police, has often proved an effective deterrent to robberies in residential areas. But one couple, Jeffrey and Denise Lagrimas of Oroville, California, probably would not have gotten involved if they had known exactly how effective the program could be.

The saga began in May of 1989, when Nanci Miller of Oroville stored home furnishings, books, and clothing in a rented self-storage locker in the town. On November 19, she discovered that thieves had broken into the locker and stolen most of her stored belongings.

Three days later, she placed an advertisement in the local newspaper, the *Oroville Mercury-Register,* describing the missing items and asking readers to call her if they had any information. One did, an anonymous caller who claimed to have seen some of Miller's furniture carried into a neighbor's house; the neighbors, the caller added, had always acted suspicious.

The caller had one other item of information: The suspect couple

was hosting a Neighborhood Watch meeting in a few days, and perhaps Nanci Miller would like to attend. Indeed she would, and did, with the cooperation of the police.

The experience was, Miller later said, like a visit to her own home. There in the living room were her television set and stereo. In a bed-room was a dresser removed from Miller's storage locker. The kitchen held Miller's dishes. Her two daughters' books stood on a shelf. And the hostess wore Miller's own skirt and blouse.

Miller, thoroughly shaken, reported her find to police. Armed with a search warrant, they turned up $9,000 worth of stolen property and a container of illegal drugs in the Lagrimases' home and in storage lockers the couple had rented—adjacent to Miller's.

The pair were charged with burglary, possession of stolen property, and drug possession. They were sent to prison on the drug charges, never revealing why they hosted the Neighborhood Watch meeting that led to their arrest. □

Try, Try Again

In the bulging register of failed plotters, Peter Anthony Scott of Southsea, England, may well rank as the supreme example of ineffectuality. Over a two-year period, the unemployed computer programmer made seven attempts to kill his wife, Bernadette. Each effort flopped so badly that the intended victim never suspected a thing.

In 1980, feeling pinched for money shortly after their marriage, the twenty-six-year-old Peter Scott took insurance policies that would pay a total of £245,000 if his wife were to die by accident. His first efforts to stage a fatal "accident" were somewhat halfhearted. On a trip to Yugoslavia, he asked Bernadette to join him in admiring the view from the edge of a sheer cliff, thinking to push her over; she, fearful of heights—or something—declined. Peter repeated the invitation again at a rocky promontory on the English coast. Bernadette again kept back from the brink.

Plainly, a more active approach was needed. Peter purchased a large amount of mercury and tried to mix it into a strawberry dessert. But the metal refused to cooperate; instead of mixing, it flowed in globules onto the plate. He recovered some of the toxic metal and added it to a mackerel dish he cooked for her a few days later. His wife ate it with gusto and suffered no ill effects.

Concluding that fire might work better than poison, Peter put a candle outside his wife's room when she was in bed with chickenpox; he kicked it over as he left the flat for the evening. Flames spread across the carpet, but a student who lived in the building arrived and doused the blaze. Three days later, Peter started a fire on the ground floor with some paper; the same student raised the alarm, and Bernadette fled to safety as flames devoured the building.

On his last attempt, Peter asked his wife to stand on the side of the road while he tested their car's suspension. He planned to run her down—but swerved away at the last instant.

After this episode, Peter visited a psychiatrist and explained, "I keep trying to kill my wife." The doctor decided that her new patient was a dangerous psychopath and alerted police, who quickly took Peter into custody. Further psychiatric examination convinced authorities that Peter had "a substantial mental disorder" that appeared to be worsening. No room was available in a suitably secure mental hospital, so he was sent to prison for an indefinite stay. Peter's wife, finding her husband's intentions toward her hard to believe, said she was "shattered." □

GANGS AND GANGSTERS

The human social instinct—that urge to join with like-minded comrades for the sake of sharing life's burdens and joys—apparently is as strong among outlaws as law-abiding citizens.

Criminals may form alliances for the same reasons as accountants or animal lovers: companionship with colleagues, protection, research and innovation, education, and the pursuit of professional perfection, to name but a few. For the criminals, however, the means to these ends are usually violent and alarmingly direct: murder, arson, bribery, and threat, for example. Even so, some gangsters have found use for the press release, for formal schooling, so that the young might better learn the craft of theft and battery, and even acquire the dedication of the meticulous criminal mastermind, rehearsing to the point of exhaustion in pursuit of the flawless heist.

Confederation does not confer invincibility. On the side of the law there are some who are not swayed by swagger or bribes. And violence cuts left and right, up as well as down—a discovery most crooks make too late, as their lives grow gray in prison wastelands or their blood drains into the dust.

Queen of Thieves

The theater was jammed with English gentry, drawn to the performance as much by the king's presence as by the drama. But the young gentleman from Yorkshire had eyes for one young, beautiful woman who dressed like a queen. And she acted like royalty, exhibiting exceptional poise and charm.

He was smitten. She was coy, gently informing him she was newly married to a jealous, suspicious man. He persisted, and finally, the dangers of early eighteenth-century London being great, she allowed him to escort her home in his carriage. During the ride, she agreed to entertain him in her home a few days hence, while her husband was out of the city. He left her at a mansion in Covent Garden.

One can only imagine his excitement when she greeted him on the appointed day. Eagerly, he tossed aside the finery he had worn to impress her—a gold watch, a gold-hilted sword, a gold-headed cane, and a heavy purse—and threw himself into her bed. As he basked in the sunshine of her smile, she warmly pressed his hand; his diamond ring slipped into her palm, and she slipped into the bed.

Moments later, the lady's maid-servant pounded frantically on the door to warn that the husband had unexpectedly returned. The beauty leaped up, donned a robe, and went to greet her husband, promising her lover to resume the tryst once the unsuspecting spouse had retired to his room. She snatched up her visitor's clothes and valuables—to hide them from her husband, she said—and locked the door behind her.

In the morning, the young man, who had spent the night alone, rang for the servants. But the household members he saw the night before were long gone, as was the lady of his dreams. In their place were the true owners of the house, outraged to find that their home had been looted. They vented their anger on the suckered swain by demanding compensation and threatening to tell the world all about his escapade if it was not forthcoming.

As foolish as he had been, the young man was not alone. He had been robbed by one of England's master thieves—Jenny Diver, she was called, queen of pickpockets, whose exploits won her fortune and notoriety by the age of eighteen. She soon became the model for a character in John Gay's 1728 play, *The Beggar's Opera*.

Jenny's real name has been lost

to time and legend. There is no question, however, that she was attractive, well-spoken, and somehow educated above her station. She had a flair for elegant dress and an acting talent that allowed her to pass as rich and wellborn. She easily mingled with members of the upper crust while she relieved them of their valuables.

Jenny was apparently introduced to the diver's trade—pickpocketing—at about the age of fifteen when her great dexterity as a seamstress was observed by the leader of a small band of thieves. Soon Jenny became the leader of her gang, and she directed its efforts where the money was.

She ignored the doings of hoi polloi, instead targeting celebrations attended by the gentry. On such occasions, Jenny resorted to ingenious techniques of theft. One involved a pair of lifelike false arms and hands. These she folded demurely in her lap, leaving her own hands free to pilfer the valuables of all around her.

Jenny Diver was good but not invincible. In June of 1738, she was sent with other convicted felons to the colony of Virginia. Within a year she was back in London, however, thanks to generous bribes to colonial officials. But in her absence, Jenny's gang had scattered, her once-nimble fingers were stiff with disuse, and she was reduced to stealing the unimposing purses of the middle classes.

Arrested again, Jenny was convicted not only of theft, but also of returning from transportation, a capital crime. On the morning of March 18, 1740, Jenny was hanged at Tyburn, London's execution grounds, and laid to rest in St. Pancras churchyard. □

Double Cross, Double Profit

Jonathan Wild, an eighteenth-century Englishman, made crime pay twice—first when he broke the law, then when he enforced it. He collected fees from gangs he organized, then turned in the least profitable crooks and collected a reward for their capture.

Wild was one of England's first supercriminals, gaining fame during his own lifetime through playwright John Gay, who used Wild as the model for the hero of *The Beggar's Opera.* Two hundred years later, Wild resurfaced as Mack the Knife in Bertolt Brecht's and Kurt Weill's *Threepenny Opera,* a musical version of Gay's play.

Wild controlled his minions ruthlessly through blackmail, perjury, and terror. Some criminologists have compared his reign to that of Chicago's Al Capone in the 1920s, only to conclude that the English crime overlord was far more vicious and surpassed even Capone in dealing out misery.

England in the 1720s was the perfect milieu for a man of Wild's moral delinquency. The government was corrupt and scandal-ridden, unemployed workers rioted, and there was talk of a conspiracy against the Crown. In London, crime was rampant. Gangs of lower-class thieves called footpads and their upscale counterparts, dubbed Mohocks, prowled lampless streets, beating and robbing pedestrians at will. Carriages and wagons were preyed upon by mounted highwaymen who swarmed over every road. There were harsh laws—more than 350 offenses merited the death penalty—but precious few enforcers. Constables had only limited authority; bounty hunters took up the slack, but only if a reward could be collected.

This was the scene that greeted the twenty-six-year-old Wild when he arrived in London to stay around 1709. He left his wife and family to fend for themselves back in Wolverhampton more than 100 miles away. Wild's London start was not promising, for he spent the first three years in debtors' ◊

A contemporary engraving depicts Jonathan Wild surrounded by records of the stolen goods he sold.

prison. However, there he made the kind of contacts that would stand him in good stead for the rest of his career. Soon after his release he owned two brothels, which became his headquarters for a profitable fencing operation. Wild contrived an ingenious scheme to avoid prosecution for receiving stolen goods and, in the process, expanded the market for his talents. Unlike earlier fences, who bought merchandise from thieves and then resold it, Wild never went near the loot. He chose, instead, to play the broker: Thieves provided Wild with detailed lists of the take from each robbery; Wild then called upon the victims, most of whom willingly paid to have their valuables returned. The cost: a finder's fee of at least half the value of the merchandise—plus a "reward" for Wild. Soon, it was no longer necessary to make house calls; Wild opened an office in one of the city's many Cock Alleys—this one just a few blocks from Newgate Prison—to receive the constant stream of robbery victims and thieves with loot to sell.

It seemed that no matter how hard the government tried, its efforts to halt the wily Wild only succeeded in enriching him. In 1718, a new law made it a felony to accept a reward for stolen property without first arresting the thieves. Wild simply obeyed the law, obligingly turning in thieves while conducting the rest of his business as usual. He got away with it. Indeed, Wild used the law to consolidate his power over the London under-

world. His secret was careful selection of his victims. Unsuccessful thieves—those deemed unlikely to contribute to Wild's pocketbook—and those who attempted to usurp his power found themselves accused of crimes, whether or not they committed them. For evidence, Wild could always produce complete and accurate lists of loot from his voluminous ledgers. The police, happy to convict anyone, went along.

Wild's Office for the Recovery of Lost and Stolen Property moved to Old Bailey, the street from which the city's criminal courts take their name, and became such a fixture that London newspapers billed their weekly crime reports as originating "from Jonathan Wild's at the Old Bailey." Wild was admired and courted by the well-to-do for his skill at catching thieves and returning stolen property. And he was obeyed by the thieves themselves because of the threat that he might turn them in. He once

boasted that he had the power to hang every thief in London.

Not quite. In 1724, Wild's system of double cross backfired when he tried his scheme on Jack Sheppard, a well-known thief in his employ. Tipped off about stolen goods, Wild fingered Sheppard and his partner, Blueskin Blake, for stealing 108 yards of cloth and two silver spoons from a drapery shop. The plan was successful: Sheppard was convicted and locked up in Newgate Prison, and Wild earned a forty-pound reward. That would have been the end of an ordinary crook, but Sheppard was a formidable opponent who loved to give interviews. Newspapers were sonn filled with Sheppard's account of the double-dealing Wild. In the public's mind the thieftaker became the villain and soon influential Londoners began to suspect they had been "taken" by Wild.

Wild was arrested in May of 1725, condemned to death for taking a reward for recovering lace that had been stolen at his instigation, and hanged at Tyburn before a jeering crowd.

Jonathan Wild is still in London, however. Graverobbers snatched his body a few nights after the execution and sold it to surgeons. His skeleton is displayed to this day at the museum of the Royal College of Surgeons of England. □

A nineteenth-century artist captured the chaos of New York's Five Points district, where domestic chores and fistfights shared the streets, and grocery stores sheltered hoodlums.

Greens and Gangsters

Rosanna Peers opened one of the first greengroceries in New York's squalid Five Points section sometime around 1825. Fresh produce was unobtainable and unaffordable to the poverty-stricken residents of the area, but spoiled or damaged produce could be purchased for pennies in Peers's front room. But the real profits were made out back, where Peers sold cheap whiskey and afforded a haven to one Edward Coleman, a petty thug with a flair for organization. In Peers's smoke-filled back room in 1826, Coleman is believed to have formed New York's first organized criminal street gang, the Forty Thieves. From Peers's parlor, Coleman sent forth killers, pickpockets, and thieves to intimidate the weak and prey upon any prosperous-looking person foolish enough to visit the thieves' domain.

The operation was so successful that it soon had imitators. More greengroceries were opened, offering the same poisonous produce—rotten vegetables out front and rotgut in back—and serving as headquarters for gangs such as the Shirt Tails, the Roach Guards, the Plug Uglies, and the Dead Rabbits. Fierce rivalry among gangs led to frequent fights that sometimes resulted in pitched battles that raged for days, using all manner of weapons, from teeth to pistols. Often, police had to call in regiments of militia to restore order.

The setting was ripe for chaos. Once, the Five Points area was known as the Collect Pond, where colonial New Yorkers boated on pleasant summer days. As the city spread north over Manhattan Island, the pond was drained and streets were built across it. The area's name was taken from the five street corners created by the confluence of three thoroughfares: Cross, Anthony, and Orange streets. The streets may have been laid out, but the area's character remained that of a swamp. Although the Five Points enjoyed a brief period of respectability, by the 1820s many of its buildings were sinking, and with them the quality of life. Irish immigrants swarmed into decaying tenements, living in abject poverty in garrets and dank cellars, eking out a marginal existence. The primary occupations were vice and crime. For some fifteen years in the 1820s and 1830s, Five Points averaged almost one slaying a day—a total of more than 5,000 murders.

To profit from the wretched immigrants, saloons, dance halls, and bawdy houses sprang up. Although greengroceries filled a need for more sustaining food, street peddlers were common. Usually, they were women and children selling mint, strawberries, hot yams, and radishes. But the calico-clad hot-corn girls, plaid shawls thrown jauntily over their shoulders and cedar-staved buckets filled with steaming roast corn hanging from their arms, drew the most attention. Coming forth at dusk to vend their wares throughout the night, they were popular with the area's young men, who battled furiously for their favors. For some of the men, the object was affection. For others, it was income, for many husbands earned their living off their wives' hot-corn sales.

In the end, it was a hot-corn girl that brought down Coleman. The gangster had battled a dozen others to win the services of one lady, now nameless. Victorious, he married her—then beat her to death because her earnings were less than he expected. That misdeed put a noose around the neck of the great-grandfather of gangsters on January 12, 1839. It also earned Edward Coleman the dubious distinction of being the first man to be hanged at the Tombs, New York City's prison. □

An 1860 membership certificate *(left)* shows quarters and equipment of the Weccacoe Fire Company (also called the Weccacoe Engine Company) in 1840, 1850, and 1860. Below is a parade hat of the rival Shiffler Hose Company.

Firefighting and Fisticuffs

Extinguishing fires in a crowded city is dangerous under any circumstances. But in Philadelphia during the mid-1800s, volunteer firefighting was closer to armed combat than it was to community service.

Prior to the 1830s, the upstanding citizens who manned volunteer fire companies made an important contribution to Philadelphia's public safety. After a time, however, political and ethnic differences intruded, turning the companies into urban hazards. What were once good-natured contests to be first on the scene and first to a hydrant became pitched battles for position and possession. Rivals on firefighting missions enthusiastically cut each other's towropes and jammed carriage wheels. Ambushes, vandalism, and theft of valuable firefighting equipment were frequent occurrences.

The situation deteriorated with the emergence of street gangs, whose members, reveling in the sheer joy of combat, ran as protective escorts for the companies, often helping pull the equipment and always joining in any scuffle. Before long, the fights evolved from brief scuffles at the scenes of fires to full-blown riots, marked by arson, gunplay, and even murder. Victory in the fighting no longer conferred the honor of putting out a fire, but control of a neighborhood; the volunteer firefighting system became the gangs' avenue to power and prestige.

A gang called the Rats became a major power in Philadelphia's Southwark neighborhood, for example, after attaching itself to the Weccacoe Engine Company. Members of another combat gang, the Killers, infiltrated the Moyamensing Hose Company during the 1840s and became the most feared group in Philadelphia. In 1849, the Killers attacked the Shiffler Hose Company and captured the Shiffler carriage. After dragging its trophy to Moyamensing, the gang ceremoniously hacked the carriage to pieces and handed the remains as mementos to an admiring crowd.

Eventually, the steam-driven pump effectively ended the violent era. The delicate, complex new machines required skilled mechanics. Fewer, better-trained professionals were found to be more effective firefighters than large numbers of unskilled brawlers. Moreover, the cost of maintaining the machines was often more than any one volunteer company could bear, and the need for cooperation brought consolidation and, ultimately, municipal financing and control.

An ordinance creating a professional Philadelphia fire department was passed in 1870. By January 8, 1871, the department went into operation. It was, according to one grateful account, "a model in every particular, a source of pride to the city, and a credit and honor to those who compose it." □

Trade School

Italian Dave, a mid-nineteenth-century New York schoolmaster of sorts, did not believe in simply giving his students bad grades for poor performance. Instead, he ceremoniously donned a policeman's uniform and beat the unfortunate bunglers with a night stick. For the homeless waifs who were his pupils, Dave's grading system had a realism afforded by no other. Like the boys in Charles Dickens's novel *Oliver Twist,* who learned nefarious skills at the knee of an evil mentor named Fagin, Dave's boys aspired to learn a life of crime. Failure in this hard school could result in far harsher punishment than their schoolmaster's whacks.

Around 1840, after a career as a working criminal, Italian Dave—his real name is now lost—set himself up as an American Fagin in a rickety tenement in Paradise Square at the center of the infamous Five Points *(page 39).* For the next twenty years, he gave daily lessons in the art of thievery. His classes averaged around forty boys, ranging from nine to fifteen years old.

The curriculum included the bread and butter of survival on the streets: effective begging, shoplifting, and the selection of likely mugging victims. But Dave's favorite activity was teaching the techniques of picking pockets. For this, he had a range of educational aids in the form of life-size fully dressed dummies that could be arranged in a variety of positions to mimic a live "mark" in the street.

Like any other, Dave's school featured field trips, on which he took to the streets with his pupils on a mugging spree. If one boy was too gentle clubbing a victim, Dave would step in to demon- strate proper technique. His students became so proficient that Dave sometimes rented them out to professional gangs, naturally keeping the rental fees for himself as a form of tuition.

The schoolmaster's brightest and best included many of New York's most famous crooks, among them one Jack Mahaney, who earned great notoriety in the latter part of the century for his uncanny prowess as an escape artist. Mahaney slipped away from New York State's famous Sing Sing prison not once, but twice. □

EDEN MUSÉE
55 West 23d St.
NEW YORK

BEWARE OF PICK POCKETS

SERIES A Nº 3.   *Pick Pocket Group.*

Trojan Hearse

One novel, if morbid, approach to gang warfare was put to use during the 1870s by a Lower Manhattan gang, the Hartley Mob. This band of murderers and robbers, one of the most vicious in New York City, used bogus funeral processions to transport stolen goods through city streets. Gang members also used the hearses and funeral carriages to carry out attacks on rival gangs. An elaborate funeral, such as the one above passing New York's City Hall, featured enough carriages and mourners to disguise a good-size fighting force.

On one notable occasion, twenty members of the Hartley Mob set out to battle a superior force fielded by one of the Five Points gangs. Dressed in funereal garments and armed to the teeth, the Hartley mobsters approached the battleground at a mournful rate. When the Five Pointers respectfully divided their own ranks to allow the "funeral" to pass, the Hartley thugs poured out of the vehicles and overwhelmed their enemies.

Although the Hartley Mob was a resourceful fighting force, it neglected to keep its political fences in good repair. Victorious on the streets, the mob was done in by police and corrupt officials who had been paid to do their job by better-connected rival gangs. □

Facility for Flackery

There is no question that the depredations of Jesse James made him the best-known outlaw of the American West. In a sixteen-year career, James and his henchmen cut a wide swath through America's midsection, from Mississippi to Minnesota and West Virginia to Texas. They robbed railroads, banks, and stagecoaches of hundreds of thousands of dollars and killed thirty-one people who stood in the way. The James gang's activities were recorded in many news items, published in the sensation-seeking papers of the times. But not all the publicity was spontaneous: One contributor to the file was a Major John N. Edwards, founder and editor of the *Kansas City Times*, who often served as the James gang's press agent.

Jesse himself had a finely tuned flair for public relations. He knew how to give reporters a good story and a sensational headline, and he was solicitous of their deadlines. Once, to make sure the newspapers got the facts on time, Jesse prepared a press release in advance of a train robbery, thoughtfully providing space for editors to enter the exact amount of the loot.

The release was handed to the train's engineer on January 31, 1874, as the gang prepared to ride away with $22,000 taken from an Iron Mountain Railroad train at Gads Hill, Missouri.

"Give this to the newspapers," Jesse ordered. "We like to do things in style." The press release, headed "The Most Daring Train Robbery On Record!" read: "The southbound train on the Iron Mountain Railroad was robbed here this evening by five heavily armed men, and robbed of ——— dollars. The robbers arrived at the station a few minutes before the arrival of the train, and arrested the agent, put him under guard, and then threw the train on the switch. The robbers are all large men, none of them under six feet tall. They were all masked, and started in a southerly direction after they had robbed the train, all mounted on fine blooded horses. There is a hell of excitement in this part of the country."

James-gang news releases were commonplace, many of them originating from the professional pen of Major Edwards, a swashbuckling soldier of fortune—(he once fought for Maximilian, the emperor of Mexico installed by France's Napoleon III)—who no doubt appreciated Jesse James's style.

James's origins also won Edwards's sympathy. Like other bandits of the time, Jesse and his compatriots had been Confederate guerrillas during the Civil War. In Edwards's view, they had been forced to adopt a life of crime by Reconstruction-era politics and bankers, who—he maintained—helped to persecute former rebels and made normal life impossible.

But underneath Edwards's sympathies lay the heart of a newsman. Helping Jesse James was good business because it made good headlines. Edwards editorialized in his own paper on behalf of James and his fellows. He also often helped the outlaw by printing Jesse's letters to the editor—after carefully polishing them.

The front page of the *Times*—and later the *St. Louis Dispatch* when Edwards went to work there—often carried news of the gang's latest exploits, glamorized and sanitized to create an image of a modern Robin Hood. Edwards was the only newsman ever to win a lengthy interview with Jesse.

James was shot in the back of the head on April 3, 1882, by Bob Ford, a new gang recruit whose own head was turned by a $5,000 reward posted for Jesse's capture. Although poet Henry Wadsworth Longfellow had died a few days before and Ralph Waldo Emerson was on his deathbed—both men were lionized by the public—it was Jesse James who captured the front pages of the nation's newspapers—still playing the press to the last. □

Outlaw Jesse James and his gang hold up a bank and a train in this detail taken from a Thomas Hart Benton mural at the Missouri State Capitol.

Blueprint for Robbery

George Leonidas Leslie, the son of a wealthy Ohio brewer, was bred for success. True to his privileged upbringing, he became an honors graduate of the University of Cincinnati, a brilliant architect, and a member in good standing of New York City's social elite. He also is remembered as one of America's most accomplished bank robbers.

Leslie and his gang are credited with 80 percent of the bank holdups in America from 1865 to 1884. Their total take was estimated at $7 to $12 million. One-third of Leslie's haul was stolen from New York City banks owned by his own upper-crust friends, to whom he was known as an independently wealthy man with the finest education and good family connections.

Leslie did all the right things to maintain the image: He patronized the best tailors, belonged to the right clubs, and regularly attended the theater. He was often seen at art exhibitions and owned an impressive collection of fine books.

Leslie seldom took part personally in the crimes he engineered. Instead, he used social contacts to gain vital information about the defenses of a bank he intended to plunder. To this he added details gleaned from architects' plans, personal observations, and sometimes information from a member of his gang who would be placed in the bank as a watchman or porter. Leslie knew not only the layout of the bank and the arrangement of its furniture, but even the type and idiosyncrasies of the targeted strongbox. To that end, he kept a collection of safes and bank vaults in a lower Manhattan loft, where he would spend days experimenting with a model that corresponded to the one he planned to empty. Preparations included exhaustive rehearsals, for which Leslie sometimes constructed a full-scale model of the designated bank's interior. Then, like a successful theatrical director, he ran the burglary team through its paces again and again—often in the dark, the condition under which the actual job frequently would take place.

Leslie's advance arrangements often involved bribery of police and politicians. He learned the value of this practice early in his career, after his first and last arrest. Hauled in for a bungled jewelry-store job near Philadelphia in 1870, Leslie got the charges quashed by using his political connections and doling out cash in the right places.

In his later years, Leslie's logistical prowess frequently brought him work as a consultant to other gangs planning bank jobs. His fees were considerable: One ring in San Francisco reportedly paid him $20,000 just to look over its plans.

Leslie's genius for stealing money did not extend to managing it. He squandered much of his cash on a succession of unsavory women, and it was probably lust, rather than the police, that brought his career to an end. One of Leslie's amours was the former girlfriend of a murderous thug named Shang Draper, who had worked on some of Leslie's robberies. Draper made known his displeasure with the relationship. Leslie persisted, and not long after, on June 4, 1884, Leslie's bullet-riddled, decomposing body was discovered at Tramp's Rock near the Bronx River. His murderer was never identified. □

Blundering Bandits

The Dalton brothers, humdrum outlaws who yearned for the notoriety of Jesse James, devised a scheme that succeeded beyond all expectations. However, fame had its price, and only one of the five crooks who executed the audacious plan lived to tell about it.

Bob Dalton, the gang leader, and his brothers Emmett and Gratton started working with another brother, Frank, in the U.S. Marshal's office in Arkansas in the late 1880s. Frank stayed on the law's side. But by 1889, Bob, Emmett, and Gratton had become outlaws. First, they committed a series of train robberies from Oklahoma to California that yielded little loot, but a great taste for fame.

Accordingly, Bob laid out a plan to produce cash and headlines: The Dalton gang would become the first in history to rob two banks in the same town simultaneously. For the site of this record-setting robbery, the Daltons chose their hometown of Coffeyville, Kansas.

Bob's plan was simple enough. On the morning of October 5, 1892, the brothers and two henchmen would ride straight down Coffeyville's main street to the brick-paved town plaza, where they would tie their horses to the hitching rail in front of the Opera House, then split up and rob the two banks, each only a few steps away from the local temple of culture. Bob and Emmett would take the First National Bank, thought to be the tougher of the two; Gratton and two other gang members, Dick Broadwell and Bill Powers, would rob the Condon Bank. Because this was their hometown and the Daltons were well-known local ne'er-do-wells, they disguised themselves with false beards and mustaches. But Bob rejected Emmett's suggestion that they reconnoiter the town beforehand. After all, they knew Coffeyville as well as it knew them.

Not quite. When they rode into town—laughing and joking like boys on a lark—they discovered that part of the main street had been torn up, and the Opera House hitching rail had been removed. They were forced to tie the horses in an alley behind the plaza. At

The bodies of four members of the Dalton gang lie under the gaze of a curious child.

last, the five gangsters, each carrying a rifle, strode toward the banks. The weapons drew no attention, but the beards were conspicuously false; an alarmed bystander, Charley Gump, called out a warning before Bob and Emmett even entered their target bank. Bob turned and shot Gump in the hand—providing every resident with confirmation that something was amiss in Coffeyville. Nevertheless, the gang members strode purposefully into the banks.

Things went smoothly for Bob and Emmett inside the First National. But at the Condon Bank, Charlie Ball, the shrewd cashier, persuaded the bandits that his safe was on a time lock and could not be opened for three minutes. As ◊

the robbers waited, citizens assembled in the town square and the streets around it, armed and ready to put down the threat to their savings. The hardware-store owner handed out guns and ammunition to those without them. When Bob and Emmett emerged from their bank, they faced a plaza full of armed men. Retreating through the bank's back door, they ran two blocks to their horses.

But their steeds were still within plain sight—and under the direct fire—of townspeople in the hardware store. Meanwhile, Gratton Dalton, Broadwell, and Powers were themselves under heavy fire inside the Condon Bank. (After the battle, eighty bullet holes were counted in its walls.) Somehow, they got out—empty-handed—and joined Bob and Emmett in the alley.

Then, one by one, the robbers went down. Broadwell, mortally wounded, mounted his horse and rode away, only to die at the edge of town. Bob and Gratton Dalton died in the alley next to Bill Powers, all riddled by the bullets of Coffeyville's townsfolk. Three citizens and a marshal also died.

Emmett, who idolized Bob, rode off, only to return moments later to assist his brother. He was felled by a shotgun blast in the back. Although he suffered a total of twenty wounds, Emmett survived to serve more than fourteen years of a life sentence in the Kansas State Penitentiary. After he got out, he married his childhood sweetheart, Julia Johnson, and sold real estate in Los Angeles until his death in 1937 at the age of sixty-five.

In the end, the raid at Coffeyville did give the Daltons lasting fame—although it was far from the glory that Bob had wanted. □

Down Underworld

The grave of nineteenth-century Australian outlaw Ned Kelly lies beneath the police garage in Melbourne, its only marker the thick slab of concrete that is the garage floor. But his memory is enshrined in the hearts of the Australian people as their greatest folk hero.

Kelly was just one of many brigands called bushrangers, who roamed the Australian countryside in the nineteenth century, holding up stores and banks, robbing travelers, and generally making ventures into the country's hostile interior even more hazardous than they ordinarily would have been. Like Kelly, many bushrangers were impoverished descendants of Irish men and women who were transported out of England as punishment for their crimes. Unwanted in the British Isles and pariahs in Australia, they turned to outlawry.

Unlike the rest of the bushrangers, however, Ned Kelly became a legend. This was not because of the magnitude or bloodiness of his crimes. Rather, Ned won renown for style and flair, and for his choice of enemies: He is remembered as the stout-hearted Irish boy who fought the oppression and tyranny of transplanted English landholders and the Irish collaborators they hired as police.

Barely into his teens, Kelly began receiving the malevolent attention of the police in the town of Benalla. Twice he was charged with minor crimes, then turned loose for lack of evidence. Finally, at the age of fifteen, Kelly spent six months in prison for assault, even though his adult victim tried

to withdraw his complaint. Soon after his release, the young Irishman was arrested and sent away for three years for the theft of a horse he could not have stolen; it was taken while he was behind bars.

Released again in 1874, Ned avoided further run-ins with the law until a visit to the town of Greta in 1877. There, four constables arrested him for drunkenness. But when the four tried to drag him to jail, Kelly resisted so strenuously that they could not overpower him, even with the help of a local bootmaker who joined in. The fracas finally was broken up by the local magistrate, who later testified for Kelly at his trial. Ned got off with a small fine.

Then real trouble started. Six months after the Greta incident, Benalla police constable Alex Fitzpatrick showed up (reportedly drunk) at the home of Ellen Kelly, Ned's mother, and tried, without a warrant, to arrest Ned's brother, Dan, for horse theft. Ned arrived during the ensuing tussle.

The constable was thrown out of the Kellys' house. But soon he was back—this time with warrants charging attempted murder against Mrs. Kelly, Dan, Ned, and others. Although she was nursing a child, Mrs. Kelly was held in jail for three months until the trial.

Fitzpatrick testified that Mrs. Kelly had hit him with a shovel and that Ned, well known as a crack shot, had fired a pistol at him three times from a distance of five feet. Somehow, said the constable, he was only grazed. Despite Fitzpatrick's implausible yarn, Judge Redmond Barry sentenced Mrs. Kelly to three years in prison. Ironically, Fitzpatrick was then fired from the police force as incompetent and untrustworthy.

Ned and Dan were never brought to trial. They fled to the Wombat Mountains in the company of two friends, Stephen Hart and Joe Byrne. They settled in a hut near Stringybark Creek to pan for gold and make moonshine, hoping to earn enough money to appeal Mrs. Kelly's sentence—and to stay out of the law's clutches themselves.

Police mounted a search for the fugitives that led to tragedy in October 1878, when four constables encountered Kelly's group and three of the lawmen were killed in a shootout. Kelly later swore the police had fired first and he and his gang were only defending themselves. Nevertheless, outraged by the killings, the Parliament of Victoria Colony enacted emergency legislation giving anyone, constable or citizen, the right to shoot the Kelly brothers on sight. A new manhunt began.

For their part, the Kelly troupe turned outlaws in earnest, holding daring back-to-back robberies of banks at Euroa and Jerilderie. The take totaled £4,000. The reward for the quartet rose to double that amount. But Kelly had acquired a popular following, and he enhanced his image by making donations to needy families in the region. Relatives and sympathetic locals sheltered the fugitives, warned them of approaching police patrols, and helped keep them at large for another sixteen months.

But Kelly's flight could not last forever. When the bandit got word that police were planning to move into the nearby town of Glenrowan and mount attacks on his camp from there, he decided to beat them to the punch.

He and his three fellow bandits rode into Glenrowan on Sunday, June 27, 1880, and herded sixty townspeople—many of them Kelly supporters—into the Glenrowan Inn. That ◊

Iron armor (left) kept Ned Kelly alive during his daylong gunfight (illustrated above) with Australian police.

night, Ned donned heavy body armor forged from plowshares and waited until just before 3:00 Monday morning, when police closed in. Kelly's small band stepped onto the inn's veranda to meet the lawmen. Ned stood ten feet in front of his men and challenged the police: "Come on," he jeered, "I'm Ned Kelly and I'm made of iron." Police bullets rang harmlessly against his headpiece and body armor. Guns blazed on both sides until Kelly tried a flanking attack on the police, dragging himself and his ninety-seven-pound suit of armor through heavy brush, bleeding from wounds in his arm and foot. A dozen police blazed away at him, their bullets striking his armor with such force that he was driven backward. But Kelly's taunts continued: "Fire away; you can't hurt me," he screamed. But they could and did. Ned was knocked down by a close-range blast from a shotgun. Before he could regain his feet, police captured him.

The battle continued long into the day, and some 500 sightseers hurried to Glenrowan to witness the epic struggle. As they watched, fifty police officers poured bullets into the inn. Joe Byrne was struck in the groin and bled to death in seconds. The hostages were finally freed, and at 3:00 p.m., police torched the inn. Later, the bodies of Dan Kelly and Stephen Hart were dragged from the embers. They were burned so badly that it could not be told how they died.

Ned was taken to Melbourne for trial and sentenced to death by Judge Redmond Barry—the same man who had sent his mother to prison. Kelly was hanged on November 11, 1880, much mourned and long remembered. □

Fashion Statement

One-Lung Curran, whose bronchial deficiency eventually hastened his death from tuberculosis, had among his distinctions the founding of a gangland fashion rage.

According to legend, Curran's mistress once complained that her amour did not have a suitable fall coat. The resourceful thug took to the streets, blackjacked the first policeman he came upon, and stole the officer's long blue coat. His sweetheart tailored the garmet smartly to fit One-Lung's muscular frame, and a tradition was born.

Eventually, the gangster owned dozens of the purloined coats, each cunningly altered and all much admired by his fellows. Before long, they too began acquiring the tunics, and for a time it was nearly impossible for a policeman to travel in Curran's territory and remain fully clothed. □

Marm's Way

The best friend a burglar could have in New York during the late 1800s was 250-pound, ferret-eyed, beetle-browed, Frederica "Marm" Mandelbaum. Marm was a fence, and during nearly half a century of service to her particular community, she established a reputation as one of the most successful receivers of stolen goods that the country has ever known.

From her combination home and office at 79 Clinton Street in Manhattan, Mandelbaum dispensed cash galore to the city's thieves in return for the proceeds of their work. Since her criminal clients were usually in a rush to convert their loot into cash, Mandelbaum could usually name her price. The result was a margin of profit so enormous that she could easily buy the entire proceeds of even the largest hauls and make handsome payoffs to those in power so that she could continue her work without harassment.

Of course, Marm did have a heart as well as a purse, although the two were closely coordinated. She thought nothing of bailing out an unfortunate crook who had been arrested—always remembering to dock his next payoff, of course. And for a time, she took in young waifs at a place on Grand Street,

where she educated them in the finer points of burglary, pickpocketing, and other crimes.

The top two floors of Mandelbaum's three-story building were the family living quarters, which Mandelbaum shared with her husband, Wolfe, and their three children. The family thrived amid an opulent decor said to match that of any New York home. Well it might, for Marm regularly purchased fine furnishings stolen from the fashionable homes of the city's aristocracy. Secure in her luxurious environment, the high-living fence entertained lavishly, staging dinners and dances that were attended by the upper crust of the criminal world, as well as by the various police officials and politicians who protected her operation. Presumably, the protection arrangement worked both ways, to some extent,

Fence Marm Mandelbaum displays stolen wares and an ingratiating smile in a contemporary engraving.

since her guests never found themselves seated on their own antique furnishings.

During her illustrious career, Marm Mandelbaum is estimated to have handled as much as $10 million worth of stolen property. She was finally indicted for grand larceny and receiving stolen goods in 1884, after doing business with an undercover Pinkerton detective. She promptly made bail for herself and two confederates, then fled to Toronto with an undisclosed amount of cash—some guessed it was a million dollars—that maintained her in some style until her death in 1893. □

One seventeenth-century London gangster known by the name of Moll Cutpurse regularly wore men's clothing. She was once punished for this offense by being put on display wearing only a sheet. Wailing loudly, Moll Cutpurse attracted quite a large crowd—convenient and easy pickings for her pickpocket colleagues.

Sticky Fingers

The Molasses Gang was a group of small-time till tappers and sneak thieves working New York City in the 1880s. In no way exceptional otherwise, the gang is memorable for the effective, if sloppy, modus operandi that gave it its name.

Gang members would sashay into a small store, where one of them would remove his soft felt hat and ask the store owner to fill it with sorghum molasses. This would settle a bet, the hat holder would tell the mystified shopkeeper, on how much the hat would hold. No sooner was the hat full than the gangster would jam it down on the merchant's head, leaving him temporarily blinded while the gangsters emptied the till and made off with everything they could carry. □

Smashing Success

Edward "Monk" Eastman *(right)*, who became one of New York's first big-time crime bosses at the turn of the century, built his success with fist and club.

Although he stood only five feet, five inches tall and weighed 150 pounds, Eastman looked as vicious as he was. At least a dozen knife scars transversed his face and neck. A bullet-shaped head set on a bull neck hosted cauliflower ears and a broken nose. A derby hat several sizes too small perched atop a shock of bristly hair.

Eastman's weapons included the blackjack and brass knuckles. But his favorite was a club whose handle bore a notch for each head it cracked. Once, after counting up forty-nine notches on his truncheon, Monk calmly walked up to an unsuspecting bystander and clouted him unconscious. "I just wanted to make it an even fifty," Eastman explained. □

Big Wheel

Near a tram stop on the rue Ordener in Paris, French anarchist and bandit Jules Bonnot and his gang pulled a robbery that gained them a tidy Christmas present and a permanent place in the history of European crime. On the morning of December 21, 1911, about nine o'clock, Bonnot and his crew of thugs ambushed a courier from the Société Générale bank. While the twice-shot courier lay mortally wounded on the street, the gang grabbed a pouch holding the loot—cash and securities—and roared off in a stolen Delaunay-Belleville automobile.

His high-speed departure, which involved a great deal of wild shooting and an additional handful of casualties, made Jules Bonnot the first European robber to use an automobile in a getaway. Thus he and his gang quickly became known throughout France as the "gangsters with wheels."

Bonnot, a stocky little man with a pug nose, was a highly skilled mechanic who could have easily made an honest living. His professed anarchism, however, pushed him into a life of violent crime. He and his band of merciless crackpots claimed to believe good and evil were artificial concepts invented to arbitrarily restrain behavior. But some felt Bonnot's philosophy was no more than an excuse for breaking out of the boredom of the quiet bourgeois life he led in Lyon between crime sprees.

Whatever his motivations, Bonnot loved cars and knew how to steal them. He and his gang stole one car after another as they made their way from robbery to robbery. On March 25, 1912, the band hijacked a car that belonged to a wealthy Parisian on the road from Paris to Nice, killing the chauffeur and his companion. The gang used the purloined automobile in a bank robbery in Chantilly, where they killed three people and fled with 50,000 gold francs.

But that was the gang's last job. Enraged by Bonnot's depredations, French authorities mounted a relentless pursuit. Three of the six men involved in the Chantilly robbery were arrested with little trouble. Bonnot remained at large.

After a bungled arrest attempt in Ivry, in which an unarmed deputy police chief was killed, Bonnot was run to ground at the estate of an eccentric millionaire at Choisy-le-Roi. On April 28, 1912, a force of 1,100 police officers and soldiers, augmented by armed civilians from the surrounding countryside, encircled Bonnot's redoubt. As many as 20,000 spectators thronged the grounds to witness the confrontation.

The siege lasted four hours. Finally, unable to dislodge Bonnot with round after round of small-arms fire, the police decided to use dynamite. Two initial explosions did little damage, but a third demolished the house and set the ruins on fire. The attackers stormed the house.

Some accounts of the battle say that the police found Bonnot dead from a self-inflicted bullet to the brain, a suicide note by his side. Another version, perhaps more consistent with the bandit's personality, has it that Bonnot was killed by police.

Whatever the truth, a passage in the note that Bonnot is said to have left bears witness to the bandit's twisted motivations. "I am a famous man," the note read, "my fame rings to the four corners of the globe, and the publicity given to my humble person must make all jealous who have put themselves to so much effort just to be spoken of." □

Badge of Dishonor

Alphonse "Scarface Al" Capone would have had the world believe that the livid scars disfiguring the left side of his face were the result of World War I shrapnel wounds. He claimed to have served with the legendary Lost Battalion of the Seventy-Seventh Division, which staged a heroic five-day battle against surrounding German forces in 1918. The story added class to a reputation that badly needed it.

The truth, however, was more consistent with Capone's life. The hulking hood acquired his facial decorations in 1917 in New York while working as a bouncer at the Harvard Inn, gangster Frankie Yale's Brooklyn dance hall. It was a foul mouth, not heroism, that earned Capone his ugly medal. One night he spoke admiringly, if crudely, about the attributes of a young lady, Lena Galluccio. She was the sister of a small-time Sicilian hoodlum, Frank Galluccio, who happened to be standing within earshot.

At 148 pounds, Galluccio was hardly a match for the 200-pound Capone, but he had no alternative other than to demand an apology for the insult to his sister. None was forthcoming. Instead, Capone attacked Galluccio, who whipped out a pocketknife and went for the larger man's throat. He missed the gangster's neck but opened wounds in Capone's face that required nearly thirty stitches.

Capone was lucky. "I was a little drunk," Galluccio would explain years later. "I think my aim was not good because of the booze." After the attack, Galluccio and his sister fled the club. A short while later he heard that "a big guy" was looking for him. But Galluccio had connections; gangsters Charles "Lucky" Luciano and Giuseppe Masseria agreed to mediate. They soon decreed that Capone should not have insulted Galluccio's sister. In effect, they informed Capone that he got what he deserved; no revenge might be taken. They ordered Galluccio to apologize for slashing Capone, and the matter was closed. □

Terrible Tommy

They called it the Chicago Typewriter or the Chopper. Firing .45-caliber bullets at a rate of 800 rounds per minute, it could empty a 100-round magazine into its victim in less than eight seconds. This was the Tommy gun: a lightweight, easily concealed, rapid-fire weapon that put roar in the Roaring Twenties and smeared blood on the streets of every major city in the United States.

Invented by General John T. Thompson and officially known as the Thompson submachine gun, this brutally efficient firearm was originally designed for trench warfare in World War I. However, the war ended before Thompson's "trench broom"—his apt, if cold-blooded, nickname—could be used by Allied soldiers. Nevertheless, in 1921, the inventor ordered 15,000 weapons to be manufactured in the hope that he could persuade someone to buy them. The military wanted none, so Thompson turned to law-enforcement officials. Again there was no sale.

By 1925, however, the gun had found an enthusiastic market among the nation's growing number of bootleggers and other mobsters seeking a better way to battle their rivals. The Tommy gun was a gangster's godsend. With a modicum of skill, a gunman could kill at relatively long range from the safety of a speeding automobile. In addition, he had little worry about return fire; targets who survived the initial volley normally dived for the nearest cover.

For all the weapon's assets, the first attempted Tommy-gun hit, on September 25, 1925, was a clownish failure. Spike O'Donnell, intended recipient of the Thompson's attentions, was standing in front of a drugstore on a busy corner in Chicago's West Englewood district. He heard someone shout his name and wisely dropped to the sidewalk just as a noisy burst took out the window behind him. O'Donnell, emerging from the wreckage unhurt, strolled into the drugstore and asked for a drink of water.

Improvements in skill eliminated such problems. Under the enthusiastic patronage of bootlegger and mobster Al Capone, a squad of Thompson-equipped assassins hit the streets of Chicago. Capone's hired guns trained in private gyms and practiced on machine-gun ranges set up in the Illinois countryside, and the training was soon put into practice. Capone's Tommy guns were the featured performers in gangland's most famous hit, the 1929 St. Valentine's Day Mas-

sacre of seven henchmen of rival hoodlum Bugs Moran.

Despite the Tommy gun's notoriety—or perhaps because of it—legitimate sales of the weapon remained slow throughout the 1920s and 1930s. By 1939, only about two-thirds of the original inventory of 15,000 had been sold, and Thompson's Auto-Ordnance Corporation was on the block. Connecticut industrialist Russell Maguire picked up the pieces for $529,000, the approximate wholesale value of the 4,700 guns still in stock.

Just weeks after the sale, Germany invaded Poland; every Allied army suddenly remembered the Thompson submachine gun and flooded Maguire with orders. The company's new owner, who became famous as America's "Tommygun Tycoon," sold more than two million of the guns before World War II ended. □

Parental Preparations

When Edward and Cecelia Cooney learned that she was pregnant, they began preparing for their first child's financial future. On January 5, 1924, they started by robbing a chain store in Brooklyn, New York.

The take was $688, an impressive sum to an unemployed auto mechanic and a laundress living in an eight-dollar-a-week rented room—enough to encourage them in their unusual form of estate planning. They set aside half the loot from their first heist for their child, then invested in a second pistol. With what was left over, Edward bought a new pair of shoes and Cecelia bought a new dress and had her hair bobbed in the flapper style.

A three-month run of petty holdups and robberies followed, catapulting the two onto the front pages of every New York paper. Cecelia became the "Bobbed-Haired Bandit." Ed was simply "her tall companion." Tailored by tabloid, they became a romantic pair. They stole only about $2,000 during their brief career, but their dashing image attracted copycat criminals who mimicked them and stole thousands more. Men and women, boys and girls got in on the act.

Most of the mimics got away. Two who did not were Clarence Wilson and Fred Martini. Dressed in knee-length skirts and bobbed-haired wigs for a holdup one night, they were soon captured because they could not outrun pursuing police while wearing high heels.

Headline followed headline, the media obsession with bobbed-haired bandits feeding on itself. ◊

Brigadier General John T. Thompson demonstrates his famous submachine gun shortly after the weapon's introduction in 1921.

Brooklyn was in an uproar. Big stores hired armed guards; smaller merchants armed themselves. And detectives who were assigned to a special 500-member "Bobbed Squad" gnashed their teeth in frustration, hampered by uncertain witnesses, some of whom described the bandit as short, some as tall.

Police officers began arresting women for no more reason than their bobbed hair.

Cecelia was fast becoming a folk hero. Then one witness observed that the Bobbed-Haired Bandit was pregnant, narrowing the pool of suspects substantially. It was time for the Cooneys to head for a friendlier climate. They chose Jacksonville, Florida, where Edward had once worked—but not before one last armed robbery. Having taken stock of their dismal financ-

es, the couple decided to hit the offices of the National Biscuit Company in Brooklyn. But it was April Fools' Day, and the joke turned out to be on them.

While Cecelia held workers at gunpoint, Edward ransacked the office. An employee tried to wrestle the gun from Cecelia and Edward shot the man twice. He survived, but the unplanned shooting—it was the first and only shot the Cooneys ever fired—cut short the search for cash. They overlooked $5,900, three times what they had earned from all their other jobs combined. Worse, a small black notebook fell from Cecelia's pocket, providing police with the pair's identity.

Cecelia and Edward took a boat to Jacksonville, arriving with just fifty dollars. News of their celebrity had preceeded them. Edward had planned to get work as a mechanic, but the next day he learned from the newspaper that police had asked garages in every eastern city to be on the lookout for him. The Cooneys were broke and starving. Their baby, Catherine, was born April 12 but died within a week in a filthy furnished room.

The couple begged a funeral from a local undertaker. But he, too, had read the newspaper, and he contacted police. The fearsome Bobbed-Haired Bandit was so weak from hunger that she and her tall companion could barely lift their weapons when police crashed through their door.

Edward and Cecelia Cooney each received ten- to twenty-year prison sentences. Freed after six years and reunited in 1931, they settled on a farm in upstate New York where they had another child, its birth unheralded by any crime wave. □

Bobbed-haired bandit Cecelia Cooney poses with her husband, Edward, shortly before their arrest in Jacksonville, Florida.

Hearts and Flowers

Prohibition-era mobsters may have killed each other with shocking disregard for civilization's conventions, but they were obsessed with propriety when it came to funerals.

Hoodlum interments in that bullet-riddled epoch were often garishly opulent affairs. Homes and funeral parlors overflowed with expensive floral offerings, and the ceremonies were attended by weepy-eyed hoods—some of whom had just had a hand in killing the dear departed.

Chicago bootlegger Dion O'Banion had one of the splashiest of all gangland plantings. His $10,000 casket, a masterpiece of silver, bronze, and white satin, was built in Pennsylvania and shipped to Chicago in a special freight car. Forty thousand people viewed O'Banion's body as it lay in state at the Sbarbaro funeral chapel on North Wells Street. An orchestra

played the Dead March from Handel's oratorio *Saul,* as the pall-bearers—labor racketeer Maxie Eisen and O'Banion's triggermen, Hymie Weiss, Bugs Moran, Schemer Drucci, Frank Gusenberg, and Two Gun Alterie—carried the fallen gangster to his last limo ride. The funeral procession, led by three bands and a police escort, included twenty-five cars and trucks hired just to carry the flowers.

At Mount Carmel Cemetery, a Father Patrick Molloy, who had known O'Banion since childhood, conducted a short service. Chicago's Roman Catholic archbishop, George Cardinal Mundelein, refused to allow the gangster to be buried in consecrated ground, although the gangster had once laid claim to a certain measure of piety as a youthful altar boy and choir member. Five months after O'Banion's death, however, his body was

moved to a consecrated plot purchased by his widow.

Mike Merlo, a respected Mafia capo who perished, remarkably, of natural causes, had died two days before O'Banion. It was O'Banion's flower shop—the scene of his own murder—that provided much of the $100,000 worth of flowers that graced Merlo's farewell. Among the orders that poured in were Al Capone's $8,000 arrangement and gangster Johnny Torrio's $10,000 tribute. Jimmy Genna paid a relatively modest $750 for his order, although his method for collecting the arrangement was certainly notable. He had his henchmen pick it up, and while they were there, they pulled the trigger on O'Banion.

The most impressive of the many floral arrangements at Merlo's funeral was a twelve-foot wax-and-flower statue of the deceased. Said to be a good likeness, the enormous figure was carried in an open car preceding the hearse. □

Birger Wars

Vain and venturesome Charlie Birger was a ruthless gangster, the leader of one of the gangs that ran the violent rural counties of southern Illinois during Prohibition in the 1920s. A veteran of the U.S. Cavalry, he was handsome and especially dashing on horseback. His looks and his riding skills, he thought, made him the spitting image of cowboy-actor Tom Mix, and he tried to cultivate the romantic image of the good outlaw—a latter-day Robin Hood who tossed coins to schoolchildren, loaned money to pay the doctor bills of his destitute neighbors, and made charitable contributions.

It was a tough image to keep in an arena unused to good works. Williamson and neighboring counties had been plagued by crime and labor strife for years. For a time, the racist, anti-Semitic, and anti-Catholic Ku Klux Klan was considered the strongest force for law and order in the region. It fought against booze, at least. But with the large and thirsty population of St. Louis available to buy illegal liquor from neighboring Illinois's bootleggers, the Klan eventually lost out to the likes of Charlie Birger and his colleagues, the Shelton brothers— Carl, Earl, and Bernie.

The Klan disposed of, Birger and the Sheltons parted ways, and soon they were themselves engaged in a bitter war. It was waged with the usual array of weapons—machine guns, pistols, shotguns, dynamite, and rifles—imaginatively augmented by armored vehicles and, on one side, a rudimentary air force.

Birger's headquarters in Crab Orchard, between Marion and Harrisburg, Illinois, was the fortified roadhouse Shady Rest, featuring foot-thick log walls and a deep basement. Submachine guns, rifles, and ammunition boxes lined the walls. Canned food sat ready for a siege, and a truck armored with steel plates stood prepared for battle under floodlights in the yard. Anyone approaching Shady Rest without the proper signal could expect a harsh challenge.

Against this formidable redoubt, the Sheltons once launched a primitive air strike, dropping three nitroglycerin-and-dynamite bombs from a small plane. The missiles missed their target and, according to one account, killed a bulldog and an eagle—but no gangsters. The two sides were fairly evenly matched, and despite the hostilities, deliveries of illegal booze continued, financing the recruitment of warriors and the bribery of local and state officials.

Finally, it was the law, not the Sheltons, that got Charlie Birger. In October of 1926, Birger threatened to kill Joe Adams, the mayor of West City

Tommy gun-toting Charlie Birger (center, outlined) commissioned this family portrait of his heavily armed gang in summer 1926.

and a friend of the Sheltons, when Adams refused to turn over the Sheltons' armored truck. In November, Adams's home was machine-gunned, then bombed, but the mayor escaped injury. But on December 12, two teenage Birger recruits, Harry and Elmo Thomasson, finally shot Adams at the front door of his home. They collected fifty dollars each. Soon thereafter, Elmo Thomasson disappeared; fearful for his own life, Elmo's brother, Harry, spilled his story to the authorities.

Birger was arrested for the Adams murder. Soon, two more bodies turned up in the area: those of state highway patrolman Lory "Slim" Price and his wife, Ethel, both of whom were on Birger's payroll. Several of Birger's henchmen were tried for Slim and Ethel Price's murders.

Birger might have joined them, but by then, he had been executed for the Adams murder. "It is a beautiful world," he announced moments before the hangman's black hood slid down over his face. The Shelton brothers survived the war. But Carl and Bernie were shot to death more than twenty years later. Earl survived a shooting in 1949, then lived peacefully—and comfortably—to the age of ninety-six. □

Buying Time

Most successful crooks know the value of directing a well-timed donation to the right government agent, but seldom have bribes purchased so much for so little as they did for the Chicago Prohibition-era beer barons Terry Druggan and Frankie Lake.

Allies of the infamous Al Capone mob, Druggan and Lake made vast amounts of money from their bootlegging franchise. The flamboyant pair often boasted that their operation was so profitable that even the lowliest gang member "wore silk shirts and rode in Rolls-Royce automobiles."

The politicians and bureaucrats who protected Druggan and Lake profited, too. In 1924, the beer barons were each sentenced to a year in prison for contempt of court. Apparently, they did not mind jail, so long as they could live there on their own terms. Payment of $20,000 to Cook County Sheriff Peter Hoffman guaranteed that their sentences were served in style. The pair spent most of their time shuttling in a chauffeur-driven limousine among fine restaurants, golf courses, shops, and the theater. Druggan spent much of his sentence in his luxury duplex with his wife. Lake, on the other hand, preferred the company of his mistress. When the rare press of

Cheerful, dapper beer barons Frankie Lake *(top)* and Terry Druggan paid jailers up to $500 for a day's freedom.

business kept them in the hoosegow, they often repaired to a cell furnished as an office.

The whole nifty arrangement came tumbling down, however, when a reporter from the *Chicago American* showed up at the jail for an interview with Druggan.

"Mr. Druggan," one jailer announced with the aplomb of a butler, "is not in today." "Then I'll talk to Frankie Lake," countered the reporter. Mr. Lake also had an appointment downtown, was the reply. Both gentlemen were expected back after dinner.

Once the story broke, Hoffman was fined $2,500 and sentenced to thirty days in jail. He was clapped in a cell by one of his own deputies. "I was only accomodatin' the boys," he allegedly complained.

"The boys" served out the brief remainder of their prison sentences behind bars. □

Country Girl

Every actress who ever played a sweet-faced, tough-talking gun moll in the movies is indebted to the beautiful and rambunctious Virginia Hill. She was perfect for the part; she had looks, brains, and grit. But Hill was no actress. She was the real thing.

Born on August 26, 1916, Hill was the oldest daughter of a dirt poor, alcoholic handyman in Lipscomb, Alabama. The family lived a hard life. Hill's mother fled, leaving Virginia in charge of nine siblings. At the age of seventeen, Hill escaped to the bright lights and promise of Chicago.

With a voluptuous figure, flowing auburn hair, and a liquid southern drawl that masked a lightning-quick mind, Hill arrived at the 1933 Chicago World's Fair full of hope and ambition. She settled for work as a waitress, first at the fair, then at a restaurant at Randolph and Clark streets. It was there that Virginia Hill met the man who would transform her life.

Joe Epstein gazed across the counter at Hill and fell deeply and immediately in love. But what Hill did for the image of womanhood, Epstein most emphatically did not do for men. A scrawny, balding, thirty-three-year-old who peered through thick glasses, Epstein was, at first glance, an unlikely suitor for this young Alabama belle. He had, however, one thing in his favor: money, more money than Hill had ever seen in her life, and more than enough to kindle romance in her heart. Before long, Hill was fairly wallowing in cash and living in an apartment provided by her myopic lover.

Virginia Hill had stepped from the shoulder of an Alabama back road into Chicago's fast lane. Mild-mannered Joe Epstein was a financial genius, a broker to Chicago's bookies, and a bureaucrat in the infamous organization of Al Capone. After putting a little polish on her back-country manners, Hill began charming Epstein's gangster colleagues at parties in Chicago and New York. She rubbed elbows—and sometimes more—with the criminal elite of the 1930s: syndicate men such as Frank Nitti, Tony Accardo, Joe Adonis, Lucky Luciano, and Frank Costello. To a man, they were impressed with Epstein's beautiful, street-smart girlfriend. To show their appreciation, they steered business his way—and attention hers. She took many of the famous hoodlums for lovers and was married at least four times—once, she claimed, to famed Las Vegas gangster Bugsy Siegel. She never did marry Epstein—but he never gave up on her, continuing to bankroll her almost until the day she died.

Hill's activities were not all romantic. By the late 1930s, she had become a bag girl for mobsters, delivering crime syndicate cash in prodigious amounts to various crime chieftains across the country. Then she began traveling to Mexico, where she helped the syndicate establish lucrative drug connections. Between chores, Hill was the toast of café society. The money she earned running errands for the mob, plus the continuing deluge of cash from Epstein, allowed her to entertain lavishly. She was a legendary tipper, sometimes leaving hundreds of dollars on a nightclub bar after taking a single drink.

Hill emerged from her dream life slowly and painfully; the

waking world was unkind. In 1947, Bugsy Siegel was shot to death in Hill's Beverly Hills mansion. She was partying in Paris at the time. In 1951, she was summoned before Senator Estes Kefauver's committee investigating organized crime. Kefauver was curious about her apparently limitless—and largely unreported—income. Hill maintained that whatever she owned had been given to her by men. She claimed to know nothing about their businesses or the sources of their money. Her testimony titillated the public and impressed the Internal Revenue Service, which calculated that she had failed to pay tax on $500,000 of income.

To escape prosecution, Hill, her husband at the time, one-time Sun Valley ski instructor Hans Hauser, and their infant son fled to South America, then to Salzburg, Austria, where they settled in 1952. The Internal Revenue Service auctioned off her stateside belongings to pay back taxes and fines, and Hill later separated from Hauser.

In the last week of March in 1966, she took an overdose of sleeping pills, walked into the snowy Austrian woods, and died. □

Qualified Endorsement

Two years after he had introduced America's first affordable V-8-powered automobile in 1932, tycoon Henry Ford received a letter from Tulsa, Oklahoma, extolling the virtues of his product.

In a letter dated April 10, 1934, the author—unskilled in spelling and grammar—wrote, "While I still have got breath in my lungs I will tell you what a dandy car you make. I have drove Fords exclusively when I could get away with one. For sustained speed and freedom from trouble the Ford has got ever other car skinned, and even if my business hasent been strickly legal it don't hurt enything to tell you what a fine car you got in the V 8-."

The glowing endorsement was signed by a celebrity who was well qualified to comment on such matters: Clyde Champion Barrow, who with his girlfriend, Bonnie Parker, had been robbing banks and businesses and shooting up citizens of the American Southwest and Midwest for two years. Henry Ford's personal reaction to the endorsement is not known. But an official of Ford's company sent a routine response to Clyde Barrow, thanking him for his "comments regarding the Ford car."

Clyde never translated his admiration into a purchase; he and Bonnie stole their Fords instead of buying them. But then, the jug-eared bandit probably could not afford even Mr. Ford's modest machines. For all their ferocity, Bonnie and Clyde earned little from their labors. Their largest haul, from a bank in Cedar Hill, Texas, netted only $1,401. Their take from the small filling stations, groceries, and lunch counters that were their usual targets amounted to $76 during one typical month. Had they not been such wanton killers, Bonnie and Clyde would have been considered more nuisances than desperadoes.

But dangerous they were. Careening down the back roads of eleven states from New Mexico, Texas, and Louisiana in the ◊

Less than three weeks after sending this letter of praise to Henry Ford, Clyde Barrow stole his last Ford V-8.

South to Michigan in the North, the pair was blamed for as many as fifteen cold-blooded murders.

If guns—one of Barrow's passions—made Bonnie and Clyde deadly, the automobile—another love—gave them mobility. By all accounts, Clyde was a superb wheelman, capable of handling cars at high speed over the rough, irregular roads of the era. His stamina behind the wheel was prodigious; he regularly clocked hundreds of miles a day over country roads that were often unpaved and rutted. The pair covered hundreds of thousands of miles during their two years of aimless wandering, virtually living in the stolen cars.

Barrow particularly liked the speed and maneuverability of the Ford V-8. The car could exceed ninety miles per hour without modification. Its relatively small size and light weight allowed Barrow to slip in and out of tight spots easily. The Ford's hydraulic brakes added to its agility on the road, as Barrow demonstrated one steaming August afternoon in Wharton, Texas, where he foiled a police ambush by slueing his Ford into a U-turn—in the middle of a bridge—and roaring safely away despite a hail of bullets.

Clyde complemented his driving skills with an uncanny ability to remember roads. Emma Parker, Bonnie's mother, said Barrow's mind was "a photostatic copy of the intricate windings where he could rush in and hide, elude capture, fade into the landscape, and become lost to sight."

Bonnie and Clyde's last ride was an epic journey, beginning in the driveway of Jesse and Ruth Warren's home in Topeka, Kansas, on April 29, 1934. Bonnie and Clyde stole the Warrens' brand-new tan-gray V-8 Ford sedan. Over the next twenty-four days, the pair covered 7,500 miles, without conducting a single holdup or murder. But law-men were on the trail, and small shreds of evidence narrowed the search. On May 23, Bonnie and Clyde hurtled at eighty-five miles per hour down a nearly deserted road near Gibsland, Louisiana, into an ambush set by a posse of Texas Rangers and local sheriff's deputies. Clyde was killed almost immediately. Nevertheless, volley after volley poured from the lawmen's guns into the car. The results disproved Barrow's rumored conviction that the Ford's strong body was a bullet stopper. There were no fewer than 184 bullet holes in the car, and a total of 80 in Bonnie and Clyde. □

Creative Crooking

Police detective James Badey *(right)* of Arlington, Virginia, found that creativity was important in working with Southeast Asian immigrants who settled in the Washington, D.C., suburbs in the 1970s and 1980s. He also learned that crooks could be creative, too.

That lesson Badey acquired in the summer of 1984, when a band of recently arrived young Vietnamese toughs began extorting money and goods from local Asian merchants. The businessmen, fearful of gang reprisals, refused to press charges or even discuss the problem. Badey got creative.

Bluffing in a manner worthy of a prime-time police drama, Badey visited the gang's leader, teenager Duoc, and explained in detail what would happen if the youngster continued his criminal activity. He further suggested it would be in Duoc's best interest to leave town—quickly and permanently.

The next day, Duoc was gone—but not without an imaginative parting shot. He had gotten the merchants to finance his departure. Soon after Badey made his threat, Duoc called on several shopkeepers, told them about the warning, and asked each victim to give him $50 to speed him on his way. Delighted to be rid of this youthful plague, six merchants complied, providing Duoc with a traveling fund of $300.

The hoodlum kept his part of the bargain and left Arlington—only to settle in Alexandria, the city next door. His travel expense: approximately $1. His profit from leaving town: $299. ☐

Mild in the Streets

Dmitri, Igor, Andrei, and their friends are like members of motorcycle gangs the world over: They affect a menacing manner, wear tattoos, carry brass knuckles, razors, and knives in their dirty clothes, and party long and hard. There are perhaps 500 like them in Moscow and its environs, belonging to gangs with names such as Cossacks and Night Wolves. They ▷

meet in parks and parking lots, drinking vodka and cognac, and talking—always talking—mostly about women and motorcycles.

Fortunately talk is cheap, for motorcycles are not, with the result that the motorcycle gangs of Russia—while they have all the trappings of bikers—have precious few bikes. The sparse number of cycles available sport brand names that would invite snorts of contempt from bikers in the United States: Jawa from Czechoslovakia and Ural from Russia. Now and then a German BMW—faded and creaking—will appear. But hardly ever is heard the irregular, loping two-cylinder bark of the real bikers' bike, the American Harley-Davidson. One such prize is ridden by Sasha Zoldastanov, the leader of the Night Wolves; his machine came to Russia with a shipment of other war supplies back in 1942.

By Russian standards, Moscow's motorcycle gangs are outlaws. By the measure of many other nations, they are merely outlandish. The bikers' chains, tattoos, leather jackets, bandanas, and Confederate flags set them apart from their fellow citizens' conformity and shabby clothing. In a society accustomed to waiting patiently in line, they are called "hooligans" and "racketeers." But usually their main offense is minor: dabbling in the booming black market for T-shirts and leather goods. One biker spent two years in jail for blinding someone in a fight. But when most are arrested, it is for driving without a license, not murder, rape, or robbery. The howls of the Night Wolves and their comrades offend some Muscovites' sense of propriety, but little else. □

INFAMOUS ACTS

Most crimes are news, not history. The reports are filed today and forgotten tomorrow, crowded out by fresh accounts of greed or depravity. No matter how vicious or ingenious, today's depredations recede before the onslaught of new ones.

But some crimes do linger, made distinctive by exceptional savagery, enormously valuable loot, or the celebrity of either victim or criminal. At times, notoriety may even be conferred subtly. Some inscrutable element triggers public passion, and a sordid event enters the realm of enduring folklore, entertaining and shocking generation after generation, and instructing each in the grotesque possibilities of human nature.

3

Passion for Poison

Criminal conduct often excuses itself by the company it keeps. "Everybody's doing it" is offered as justification by cookie-snatching children and vile murderers alike. It is a poor defense, of course; that there are other thieves and killers abroad does not excuse the one who gets caught.

Thus, when the marquise Marie Madeleine d'Aubray de Brinvilliers told a court in 1676 that Parisian society was rife with poison plots, the judges dismissed her words as self-serving rant. After all, at the time, the marquise was on trial for poisoning her father and two brothers. She was duly beheaded, and her assertions were ignored.

Three years later, however, events proved that the late noblewoman had spoken the scandalous truth. The notorious goings-on reached nearly to the throne of King Louis XIV and threatened his reputation, if not his life. The cover-up he ordered saved the Sun King's nefarious courtiers and nearly buried the story from the sight of future generations.

If she was not the prototype, the marquise de Brinvilliers was typical of those who were later exposed. Hard-pressed to maintain her ex-travagant lifestyle, in 1666 the marquise and her lover, Godin de Sainte-Croix, decided to kill her wealthy father, Antoine Droux d'Aubray, so that the marquise could, along with her two brothers, inherit the old man's wealth. It was a plot that pleased Sainte-Croix; d'Aubray had had the lover imprisoned once to keep him away from the marquise. With the help of a friendly alchemist named Glaser, Sainte-Croix obtained a supply of compounds containing arsenic.

Before administering the fatal dose to her father, the marquise decided to run some tests. To this end, she became a volunteer at some of Paris's charity hospitals. There the lovely, caring noblewoman was to be found by the sides of the sick, offering sympathy, compassion, and various delicacies—laced with the arsenic-rich recipes provided by Glaser. The patients died, the marquise pronounced the alchemist's potions efficacious, and soon papa had left behind the heavy cares of the mortal world.

The marquise mourned his death and welcomed the legacy. She exhausted the money within four years but held on to her supply of Glaser's magic potions. Soon she put them to use to finish off her brothers so that she could obtain her father's money from their estates. The marquise, feigning great grief, was never suspected. But in 1672, after the untimely death of Sainte-Croix, police who thought the death suspicious were examining his possessions when they found a curious red leather chest. Inside were vials of poisons and a packet of letters from the marquise de Brinvilliers implicating the couple in the d'Aubray family deaths. Soon she was put on trial, and it was then that she revealed that "half the people I know—people of quality—are involved in this same kind of thing."

Although officially ignored, her statement started uneasy murmurings. Rumors flashed and flowed until, three years after the marquise's execution, it became clear that she was right: All sorts of seemingly upright folk, from common workers to the elegant courtiers of Louis XIV had taken up a new hobby: poisoning. Serving their needs was a coterie of fortune tellers and priests and priestesses of black magic. Anyone with a reason, be it jealousy, love, greed, or revenge, could obtain from them the potions or pills to effect the demise of another.

When the king caught wind of the scandal, he ordered the lieutenant general of police in Paris, Nicolas de la Reynie, to round up the offenders and bring them to justice. Reynie did just that—arresting, among others, the king's own mistress, the marquise de Montespan. It was said that she had not only taken part in Black Masses and attempts to poison her rival, Mademoiselle de Fontanges, but that she had even tried to poison the king himself.

On learning that bit of news, the king ordered a cover-up. The effect was that neither his deadly mistress nor other members of the court were prosecuted. Suspects less well connected were less fortunate. During a three-year investigation, more than 200 people were arrested, 34 were hanged or burned to death, a like number were fined or banished, and 4 were assigned to the galleys—a sentence equivalent to death. Most of those prosecuted were suppliers of poisons and makers of spells and other instruments rather than the noble plotters. In 1709, Louis XIV ordered all records of the tribunal to be burned. But the story survives in the private notes of Reynie, which are now preserved in the Bibliothèque Nationale in Paris. □

Tooth in Lending

Dr. George Parkman was a wealthy Boston physician and landlord of the 1840s who was generous with his money. He donated the property on which stood the prestigious Massachusetts Medical College—now Harvard Medical School—and gave freely to neighboring Harvard University. Ordinarily, his altruism might have earned Parkman a modest place in local history. But with the making of a loan to colleague Dr. John White Webster, Parkman was consigned to a premature death—and fame as the unfortunate victim in the first American crime to attract nationwide attention.

The case had all the right scandalous elements: an eminent, wealthy victim; a respected and prominent accused killer; motives of money and greed; and detectives who displayed flashy forensic footwork in solving the case.

Webster, a professor of chemistry and mineralogy at the medical college, lived beyond his means. At one point he borrowed $400—a substantial sum in those days—from Parkman. Soon thereafter, Webster sold off his highly regarded collection of minerals for $1,200 but failed to repay any of the loan. Apparently, Parkman thought that he should get his money back, and he began badgering his colleague. His demands were ignored until November 23, 1849, during a stormy meeting in Webster's laboratory. Parkman once again demanded payment. Webster answered by clouting his creditor over the head with a piece of kindling wood, killing him. His role as debtor concluded, Webster reverted to his role as anatomist. Taking up an ordinary kitchen knife, he proceeded to slice Parkman into pieces small enough to fit into the laboratory stove. He did not burn all of the parts, however; some he saved in a dissecting vault for teaching and research. ◊

A Boston caricaturist captured Dr. George Parkman as he strode Boston's streets shortly before his murder.

The disappearance of the prominent Parkman caused a great stir, not only in Boston but in the nation, as the newspapers took up the case. The papers of the day were just beginning to find a mass market and to exploit it with sensational stories. The apparent foul end of Parkman served them well, and editors clamored for police to find the doctor and the callous beast who had done him in.

The crime's solution came from a janitor at the medical college. His suspicions aroused when Webster gave him a Thanksgiving turkey—an uncharacteristically generous act by the perpetually indebted Webster—the man snooped around the professor's laboratory until he found several bones and body parts that caused him to call police. Authorities soon uncovered more body parts, and Webster was hauled off for questioning.

Webster denied everything, and he might have gotten away with the deed had it not been for the developing science of forensic medicine, the application of medical knowledge to solving crimes. Even though circumstantial evidence pointed in his direction, no one had actually seen Webster murder Parkman.

But one circumstantial item proved persuasive. Amid the ashes of the stove into which Webster had fed the pieces of Parkman's body, officers found a set of false teeth. They were Parkman's—positively identified by the dentist who served both Parkman and Webster. The gentleman wept in court as he fitted the teeth into the mold from which they were made.

John White Webster was hanged on August 30, 1850, the first American murderer to be convicted by dental evidence. □

In midnineteenth-century France, a game of billiards took a deadly turn when an argument broke out between two players. To settle their differences, the men agreed to fight a duel, using a billiard ball as a weapon. The first hurler hit his opponent in the forehead, killing him on the spot.

Hell's Belle

Belle Gunness believed in marriage; she had two husbands. She believed in insurance; after her spouses' deaths and other losses, various policies paid off handsomely. And she believed in the power of advertising; she used it to attract a number of suitors, each of whom mysteriously disappeared. But when her misdeeds began forming a noose around her own substantial neck, Belle Gunness deserted her beliefs and her home, leaving behind a barnyard full of bodies and a heap of unanswered questions.

Gunness was born in Norway in the 1860s. She arrived in America as a child and took up residence in Indiana. Many details of her life are indistinct. But by the time she reached her early forties, after the turn of the century, she weighed 300 pounds and had lived an eventful life.

She said her first husband had died of a heart attack. The proceeds from two insurance policies that she carried on his life made her a good catch for a second spouse. Unfortunately, that gentleman succumbed to an errant meat cleaver—an accident, she said. He, too, was heavily insured. Likewise, Belle carried adequate insurance on her home—a good thing, too,

for it burned to the ground after her second husband's death.

Thrice compensated, Belle bought a farm in La Porte County, twenty-five miles west of South Bend, Indiana, sometime around 1907. She moved in with the three children she and her first husband had adopted and a handyman, Ray Lamphere. The neighbors later attested to the fact that Lamphere was a hard worker, being seen frequently digging in the hogpen and elsewhere around the barnyard.

The hired man was also rumored to be Belle's lover. If so, it was a complicated affair, for although Belle had forsworn marriage, she went out of her way to be courted. Through a succession of newspaper advertisements, she sought the acquaintance of "a gentleman equally well provided, with a view to joining fortunes" on her farm. Suitors came, but few left. Most arrived with money in hand to pay off the farm mortgage and finance expansion.

One was a South Dakota farmer named Andrew Heldgren. Soon after answering Belle's ad, he began exchanging letters with the widow Gunness. Belle wooed and wowed Heldgren, writing in one missive: "My heart beats in wild rapture for you, My Andrew, I love you. Come prepared to stay forever." He did, they opened a bank account with the $2,900 he brought with him, and Andrew vanished.

But Andrew's brother, Asle, started asking questions. Belle responded by implying that Andrew had deserted her. However, Belle also told Asle that if he would visit the farm, she would help search for the missing brother—if she were paid for her trouble.

Before Asle arrived, in April of 1908, Belle's house burned (she seemed to have a taste for combustible lodgings), and four bodies were removed from the charred remains. Ray Lamphere, who by now had fallen

out with Belle, was arrested for arson and murder. Three of the bodies were unquestionably those of Belle's adopted children. The fourth was assumed to be Belle's. Although there was no head, her dentures were found nearby. But there were doubts; this body had nothing like Belle's bulk, leading to a suspicion that Belle had murdered her children and faked her own death. What was lacking was a motive for her to do such a thing.

Then Asle Heldgren arrived and made a discovery that quickly brought matters to a head. Beneath the hogpen where Lamphere the hired man was often seen digging was a graveyard. It contained the remains of Andrew Heldgren and eight more of Belle's suitors. Other bodies were found elsewhere on the farm—as many as forty, according to some accounts.

Although the evidence now tilted toward Belle's guilt in killing her children, setting fire to her own house, and fleeing, Lamphere was tried and found guilty of arson. He died in jail a year or so later.

Soon thereafter, a local minister, the Reverend E. A. Schell, announced that Lamphere had confessed on his deathbed that he had helped Belle bury her victims over the years. According to the preacher, there were also these revelations in the hired man's confession: The headless body in the burned house was not Belle's, but that of a woman who had been killed so that Belle would be presumed dead and could flee with her accumulated riches. Lamphere had agreed to help burn the house in return for a cut of the fortune—but Belle skipped off without paying.

The handyman estimated that Belle's various schemes and murders had netted more than $250,000 over the years. She was never found. □

Belle Gunness and her children posed for a family portrait four years before she disappeared and her youngsters died in their burning home.

Twisted Triangle

It was a limpid June night in 1906, and in the Garden Theater, atop New York's grand old Madison Square Garden, a dull performance of the musical comedy *Mam'zelle Champagne* was staggering uncertainly toward its conclusion. The patrons dining at stageside seemed unconcerned with the play's mediocrity. They were the wealthy and would-be wealthy of New York, there to be entertained mostly by the presence of one another. They were not disappointed.

As a singer wrapped up a tune called "I Could Love a Million Girls," the real drama started. Three gunshots rang out; there was a stunned pause, and a crashing and smashing of crockery and glasses at one of the tables. Another momentary silence followed, then a murmur of shocked recognition: Stanford White, millionaire architect and darling of Gotham's glitterati, slumped across the table as blood drained from a bullet wound in his head.

White's assailant was no less prominent. Standing triumphantly near the victim's body was Harry K. Thaw, millionaire playboy scion of a Pittsburgh railroad family. Holding a pistol high above his head, Thaw coolly addressed the corpse: "You'll never go out with that woman again."

"That woman" was Evelyn Nesbit, a show girl possessed of great beauty and meager talent, who was married to the murderer and mistress of the murdered. As hysteria swept the audience, Thaw turned to Nesbit and said, "Kiss me, dear, before I go downstairs." Nesbit smothered her husband with kisses, and a police officer escorted Thaw onto a waiting elevator.

Having thus riveted the attention of the law and the public, Thaw and Nesbit proceeded to make the most of center stage. Revelations of excess piled atop one another as the playboy and the show girl aired the details of their private lives.

Both Thaw and White were victims of Nesbit and her charms, it seemed, and she was the victim of their ambitions. In 1899, when she was only fourteen, Evelyn Florence Nesbit was brought to New York from Pittsburgh by her mother, Mrs. Winifield Nesbit. Apparently, the mother hoped that Evelyn's beauty would be the family's ticket out of poverty, and she shuttled the girl from producers to agents, seeking stardom for her daughter.

Nesbit landed a few jobs posing for calendar and magazine illustrators, and these led to a role in a dancing sextet in the popular variety show *Floradora*. There she was discovered by forty-six-year-old Stanford White, an avid theatergoer and lover of women. In her testimony at Thaw's trial, Nesbit told how the distinguished White seduced her within the first year of their acquaintance. Gifts of money and trinkets eased whatever guilt the young girl might have felt and so did the tacit approval of her mother. Mrs. Nesbit was quite pleased to take White's money to finance visits to her home in Pennsylvania, while the architect "chaperoned" the teenager through café society. The public was titillated by Evelyn Nesbit's account of awakening, naked and (she claimed) horrified, in a bed surrounded by mirrors after a night of champagne and dancing. Her horror soon diminished, apparently, for she continued her liaison with White until his death. They often shared his "pleasure house," a penthouse suite at Madison Square Garden where White entertained Nesbit by pushing her in a delicate red velvet swing.

There was evidence that to White, the architect of such landmarks as New York's Washington Square Arch at the foot of Fifth Avenue and of Madison Square Garden itself, Nesbit was not simply a beautiful, pliant young woman but the raw material for a living sculpture, animated clay that could be molded into a creature of his own imagining.

Harry Thaw's designs for Nesbit were less ambitious and certainly less noble. At thirty-four, he was a spoiled, self-absorbed ne'er-do-well who showed off by lighting cigarettes with ten-dollar bills. Privately, he was not just obnoxious but dangerous; he was known to beat his female companions. He avoided the consequences by making large payoffs to his victims. New York socialites called him Mad Harry.

Nesbit met Thaw about three years after starting her liaison with White. She accompanied the younger man on a European vacation, and he promised to marry her when they returned. Instead, he beat her during and after the sojourn. Told about the abuse by Nesbit, White encouraged her to file a complaint against Thaw. True to form, the playboy paid her to be quiet—enough so that she was also persuaded to take Thaw back into her heart, or at least into her bed. They were married, and life continued for all, virtually unal-

tered by events: Thaw beat Nesbit and conducted numerous affairs with other show girls, and Nesbit continued her affair with White. It was a classic triangle, with a classic denouement, and New York's population eagerly lapped up every detail that was printed before, during, and after Thaw's three trials.

As he had many times before, Thaw applied his family's wealth to his legal problem, obtaining the counsel of five lawyers. One, Delphin Delmas, conjured up a novel defense, in which it was claimed that Thaw had fallen victim to a mental disorder the lawyer dubbed dementia Americana. The condition, it was explained, afflicted only the American male, causing its victim to feel justified in killing any man who violated his sacred relationship with his wife. The jury—either impressed or mystified by this fictive ailment—returned a

split verdict, forcing a second trial at which Thaw was found innocent by reason of insanity. Protesting that he was both innocent and sane, Thaw was committed to an asylum for the criminally insane. In 1913, he escaped by bribing a guard but was soon captured in Canada. Brought to trial a third time in 1915, Thaw was found to be sane—and not guilty.

His marriage to Evelyn Nesbit ended in divorce, although they reconciled briefly during the 1920s. For the most part, Thaw continued to exercise his proclivity for violence and for paying off his victims when they threatened legal action. A heart attack finally killed him in 1947 at the age of seventy-six. Nesbit, who struggled through bad jobs, depression, and a suicide attempt, finally retired to California to paint seascapes. She died there in 1967 at eighty-two. □

Zapped

Dr. Hawley Harvey Crippen was a mediocre British physician with looks and personality to match: He was five feet four, shy, unassuming, and spiritless. His wife, Cora—better known as Belle—was a blowzy and domineering woman, a small-time singer who futilely aspired to opera. She overwhelmed her mousy husband, while he fell short of her demands and expectations. After enduring seven years together in New York and London, both sought diversion. Belle took up with a succession of lovers, and

the doctor began warming to his newly hired young bookkeeper and secretary, Ethel Le Neve.

Crippen, then in his late forties, and his delicate twenty-four-year-old mistress met clandestinely for nearly three years. But apparently the secret brush with youth and sweetness was not medicine enough for the doctor. What ailed him was his wife, and he decided to treat her: In February of 1910, Crippen administered an enormous dose of hyoscine. This hypnotic drug, derived from the deadly nightshade plant, is a sedative in a portion of one-hundredth of a grain. Crippen gave Belle five grains, then carried the body to the basement of their north London home. He sliced the ample flesh from her bones with a surgeon's skill and buried the dissected carcass in quicklime. That done, Crippen had a death notice printed for his wife, and he took up housekeeping with the demure and adoring Ethel Le Neve.

The disappearance of Crippen's wife stirred the suspicions of Belle's friends, and at their behest Scotland Yard Chief Inspector Walter Dew paid Dr. Crippen a visit. Panicking, Crippen devised a new story. His wife was not dead after all, Crippen told Inspector Dew.

On the contrary, the concupiscent Belle was all too alive—run off to America with one of her lovers. Crippen could not bear the humiliation of admitting the awful truth, he said, and so he concocted the story of her death.

The law remained unconvinced, so Crippen thought to escape England for Canada aboard the ocean liner *Montrose* on a summer's day in 1910. Ethel accompanied him, disguised as his young son. Crippen was clearly a master at self-deception, for the attempted ruse fooled almost no one who saw the couple. They displayed an affection for each other that was anything but filial. Moreover, even in baggy boy's garb, Ethel was, in certain respects, distinctly female.

With Crippen's disappearance, Scotland Yard's skepticism turned into outright suspicion, and the public was alerted that the doctor and his young friend were fugitives. Armed with that information and his own outraged suspicions about the pair, the *Montrose*'s captain, H. G. Kendall, launched himself and Crippen into a minor role in the history of technology.

At mealtimes, Kendall entertained Crippen and his "son" at the captain's table, describing the wonders of the magical wireless radio that had just been installed aboard his ship. Between meals and at night, Kendall used the same wireless to send dispatch after fascinating dispatch on the doctor's whereabouts and activities to authorities in London. As Crippen and his lady carried on their masquerade, blissfully unaware of what newfangled science was doing to them, their unmasking was detailed at length by newspapers in America and Britain.

A more immediate threat to Crippen's dreams of happiness, Scotland Yard's Inspector Dew pursued the milquetoast murderer aboard another ocean liner, the speedy *Laurentic,* which overtook the *Montrose* shortly before she was to dock in Quebec. Crippen and Ethel were lured on deck by an invitation from the *Montrose*'s captain to watch the harbor lights. Soon Inspector Dew and a party from the *Laurentic* came aboard and arrested the astonished pair.

Crippen, the first criminal to be captured with the help of radio, was returned to England, where he was convicted and hanged for Belle's murder. Ethel, charged as an accomplice, was acquitted. □

Criminal Circus

In the early 1930s, Charles and Anne Morrow Lindbergh were the personification of America as its people wished it were. The country, then in the midst of the Great Depression, was drab, worn, and fearful. The Lindberghs were young, brave, and beautiful. Moreover, they were likable. Charles was, of course, the daring Lone Eagle, who completed the world's first solo flight across the Atlantic in 1927. Anne was a popular writer and the daughter of a wealthy New Jersey family. They had married in 1929, and their son, Charles, Jr., was born a year later. Charles, Sr., had never lost his boyish shyness; he surrounded himself with family, an estate in northern New Jersey, and a pleasant shell of privacy. While others in their position may have glittered, flaunting their wealth and fame, the Lindberghs glowed with a warm flame.

The flame was extinguished on March 1, 1932, when a kidnapper using a rickety ladder to reach a second-story bedroom snatched little Charles from his bed. The act infuriated the public and focused its unwavering attention on the crime and its gaudy aftermath.

The reaction to the crime by the New Jersey State Police—led by Colonel H. Norman Schwarzkopf, Sr.—was neither swift nor certain. To be sure, officers were flooded with unsolicited leads; sightings of children and suspicious-looking adults were reported throughout the nation. No matter how silly each seemed, it had to be run to ground. And the state and local police had little help; the FBI had

no authority to intervene. One of the few constructive results of the case was passage of the so-called Lindbergh Law, allowing federal law enforcement officers to pursue kidnapping cases.

Suspects proliferated. Each detail, real or imaginary, no matter what its source, was duly reported by newspapers. And the desperation of the Lindberghs—to find their child and to end the excruciating publicity—was palpable. ◊

Bruno Richard Hauptmann was photographed at New York police headquarters three days after being charged with kidnapping young Charles Lindbergh, Jr.

In this unfortunate atmosphere, cruel con artists and connivers flourished and rubbed elbows with the merely misguided and the well-intentioned.

A mysterious figure who called himself "John" offered to lead the Lindberghs to their son in return for $50,000. With the help of Dr. John F. Condon, a family friend and retired teacher, the ransom was paid, and Charles Lindbergh went on a wild goose chase to the island of Martha's Vineyard, Massachusetts, where John claimed the boy was hidden. The father returned empty-handed.

Mobster Al Capone, then in jail for tax evasion, offered a $10,000 reward for the baby's return. He also volunteered to tap his underworld connections to locate the kidnappers in exchange for his freedom. Lindbergh and the government turned him down.

Then a rich adventurer named John Hughes Curtis of Norfolk, Virginia, got into the act. Starting harmlessly—if ghoulishly—by gathering friends in an amateur detective club to think up solutions to the crime. The club soon began conducting real searches for the child. Police stopped his activities when Curtis began holding press conferences and spinning yarns about meeting with the kidnappers.

Suspects at one time or another included virtually everyone who had contact with the family. The Lindbergh baby's nurse, Betty Gow, was questioned. So, too, was the family's English-born maid, Violet Sharpe. Sharpe committed suicide by drinking poison; some said she was driven to despair by the incessant attentions of police and press.

One of the costliest and most dramatic of the frauds involved the legendary Hope diamond; its owner, eccentric Washington socialite Evalyn Walsh McLean; and Gaston B. Means, a former FBI agent whose reputation had been tarnished by service to the corrupt administration of President Warren G. Harding. McLean was heiress to a mining fortune, and her estranged husband, Edward Beale McLean, owned the *Washington Post* newspaper. With Lindbergh's permission, McLean hired Means to investigate the kidnapping, handing over $100,000 to be used as ransom bait, plus $4,000 for Means's own myriad expenses.

Gaston Means, whose smooth

From a stand inside the courthouse where Bruno Hauptmann was tried for kidnapping the Lindbergh baby, a peddler hawks grisly souvenirs—replicas of the ladder used in the kidnapping.

talk was matched only by his criminal mind, took the $104,000 and asked for more. McLean's wealth and gullibility were finite, however; she cut Means off and saw him sentenced to fifteen years in prison for fraud. However, Means's scam created a shortage of cash in the McLean household, which she chose to remedy by hocking the Hope diamond. The 45.5-carat stone, now the property of the Smithsonian Institution and valued at more than $100 million,

was the collateral for a loan of $36,500 from New York pawnbroker William R. Simpson.

The body of Charles Lindbergh, Jr., was found in a shallow grave in Hopewell, New Jersey, two months after he was kidnapped. Nearly two years later, on September 18, 1934, a trail of bills from the ransom payment to "John" led to the arrest of Bruno Richard Hauptmann, a carpenter with a record for burglary in his native Germany.

The arrest only intensified the

sideshow. At Hauptmann's trial, throngs jammed the circuslike grounds outside the courthouse; peddlers sold snacks and drinks, but some were hawking mementos such as a tiny replica of the ladder used to make away with the child.

Hauptmann was executed for murder and abduction on April 3, 1936. Already, the Lindberghs had escaped from the notoriety of their son's kidnapping. Symbols of what was best in America, they moved to England in 1935. □

Unfortunate First

Gustav Blair admires portraits of young Charlie Ross and his brother Walter shortly after an Arizona court affirmed Blair's claim to be the real Charlie, who was kidnapped sixty-five years earlier.

Kidnapping became a fund-raising staple of American gangsters in the 1920s and 1930s. But it was virtually unknown earlier in the history of the nation. The first apparent abduction for money occurred in 1874, when four-year-old Charlie Brewster Ross was lured from his parents' yard in Germantown, Pennsylvania, and held for $20,000 ransom. Fortunately, the case had an ending that was happy—if long delayed. Because police felt payment of ransom would only encourage other kidnappers, Ross's family never paid the money demanded for Charlie, although negotiations continued in the hope the kidnappers could be arrested. Five months after the crime, the abductors were shot during a bungled burglary in Brooklyn, New York. One man was

killed outright. The other, mortally wounded, gasped out a confession—and the assurance that the child was still alive. But the youngster remained missing and was presumed dead.

Within a few years, all sorts of people began claiming Charlie's identity. Eventually, the number mounted to more than 600, many motivated by the $469,000 trust fund the elder Ross had established for his three children.

Finally, in 1939, despite the objections of the Ross family, a sixty-nine-year-old carpenter from Phoenix, Arizona, was acknowledged by an Arizona court to be the real Charlie Ross. Gustav Blair testified that in 1908 his adoptive father, Lincoln C. Miller, told him that he was Ross—and that Miller had been in charge of minding the youngster in the kidnappers' cave hideout. Blair spent thousands of dollars establishing his identity.

After the court acted, Ross/Blair traveled with his wife to Pennsylvania, where the couple remarried under his new name. He insisted that he wanted no part of the Ross money and died in 1943 at the age of seventy-three. □

Passion in the Parish

Illicit lust was probably the last quality that parishioners who knew them would have associated with the pair—he a paunchy, balding, forty-one-year-old Episcopal minister, she the lead soprano in the church choir, both of them married, and not to each other. Yet the two apparently shared an abiding passion, right up until the night they were murdered.

The minister was Edward Hall, rector of St. John the Evangelist Church in New Brunswick, New Jersey. He had been married for eleven outwardly placid years to Frances Hall, a descendant of the founders of New Bruns-wick's huge Johnson & Johnson medical products company. The cleric's unlikely inamorata was prim and petite Eleanor Mills, thirty-two, whose quiet, meek husband was the church's sexton.

On Thursday night, September 14, 1922, Hall and Mills were murdered on lonely De Russey's Lane in New Brunswick. Their bodies, which were discovered two days later by a strolling couple, looked as though they had been arranged by a sneering stage designer. The two lay side by side beneath a crab apple tree, appearing on casual inspection to be peacefully sleeping.

Their clothes were neatly arranged. Mills's face was shaded by a scarf, Hall's by a Panama hat. The minister's glasses were perched properly on his nose, and his clerical collar was precisely in place. But a closer look revealed that both had been shot, and Eleanor Mills had been badly mutilated, her throat slashed and her tongue and vocal cords removed. The killer clearly intended that the once-warbling soprano would sing no more. Strewn around the bodies were copies of the couple's love letters, lustful epistles in which the minister—"Babykins" to his beloved—and his "Gypsy Queen" hotly anticipated each new encounter. Hall's calling card was propped at his feet.

The murders took a firm and instant grip on the public psyche, partly for their gruesomeness, but mostly for their aura of holiness brought low. Almost at once, the idyllic peace of the couple's last trysting place was shattered by hundreds of souvenir hunters, who raced to grab a piece of local history. Many brought knives to chip away at the crab apple tree, which, by the end of the first day, had all but disappeared. Hot dog and popcorn vendors sprang up to serve the sensation-hungry crowds. Any evidence that might once have surrounded the bodies was soon trampled, a fact that confounded later efforts by the prosecution.

Jealousy and vengeful anger seemed likely motives for the killings, but when the obvious suspects—the spouses—were interviewed by the police, both professed ignorance of the affair, much less the murders. For a while, Mrs. Hall's two brothers, Willie and Henry Stevens, were suspected, but there was no hard evidence against them. The Somerset County grand jury spent five days listening to sixty-six witnesses before concluding that there was no one to charge with the murders. The case languished for four years.

Then, in 1926, Frances Hall and her brothers were suddenly arrested and brought to trial. The principal evidence against them was supplied by Jane Gibson, a thrice-married divorcée who ran a hog farm near the scene of the murders. Four years earlier, Gibson had claimed that she witnessed the killings, but she had been able to

furnish only the sketchiest details about what she saw. At the time, the press had dubbed her the Pig Woman. Now, her memory somehow refreshed and refurbished, the Pig Woman promised to tell all.

By the time the trial opened in November of 1926, Gibson had contracted cancer and was hospitalized in Jersey City. Nevertheless, she made her promised appearance. She was transported to the courthouse in a police-escorted ambulance and delivered her testimony from a portable bed. Her recollection of the night of the murder was indeed remarkable, and the Pig Woman furnished an elaborate account of events, featuring all three defendants arriving at the crab apple tree by car and leaving some time later.

Gibson's dubious credibility was in no way bolstered by her mother, who, during her daughter's testimony for the prosecution, sat at the defense table a few feet away. From that vantage point, the mother chanted at regular intervals throughout her daughter's account: "She's a liar, she's a liar, she's a liar!" As the Pig Woman was wheeled from the courtroom after testifying, she rose up from her bed and screamed her response: "I told the truth, so help me God!"

The jury did not think so, and found the three defendants innocent. Mrs. Hall continued to attend her deceased husband's church and lived quietly for two more decades. The murders remained unsolved. □

Satan's Smuggler

During the Nazi occupation of Paris in World War II, the City of Light was thrust into darkness, and there began a shadowy and ambiguous time when patriots of the Resistance broke the law and traitors—those who collaborated with the occupiers—upheld it. This was a climate in which the likes of Dr. Marcel Petiot—later known as Doctor Satan—thrived.

Although he had been a minor local official in his home region of Yonne, Petiot arrived in Paris sometime in the mid-1930s under a cloud of unspecified scandal. He set up his practice in the bustling, commercial rue Caumartin, apparently specializing in illegal abortions. After the Germans occupied Paris in June 1940, he developed a profitable sideline writing prescriptions for drug addicts, whose normal sources of supply had been cut off by the occupiers. The doctor became wealthy and began dabbling in real estate.

In 1941, Petiot bought a small town house at 21 rue Lesueur in the fashionable Étoile area of Paris and had it renovated. At about the same time, under the pseudonym of M. Eugène, he circulated word that he was a member of the Resistance and would help spirit Jews and others out of France and away from the clutches of the German secret police, the Gestapo. Before long, visitors began arriving in Eugène/Petiot's courtyard on rue Lesueur, bearing suitcases and the hope that the doctor would help them escape the Nazis.

The services were not cheap. After all, he told each would-be ◊

refugee, money was needed to pay bribes, create false documents, and compensate the doctor and others for the risks they took. No fee was fixed, but Petiot accepted jewels, silver, and any other valuables his frantic clients could offer. He was said to have made millions. Once business was out of the way, each client was given an inoculation that was required, the doctor said, by the destination countries. Invariably, the injections freed Petiot's patients not only from the dangers of wartime France but from all the cares of the world. The doctor gathered up the valuables, then turned his attention to his victims' bodies. Some he dumped in the cellar and sprinkled with lime. Others he cut into pieces and scattered during bicycle rides in the country. Some he burned, sending up a putrid smoke from his chimney. Altogeth-

er, Petiot led sixty-three victims to their death—Jews, anti-Nazis, drug addicts and dealers, criminals, prostitutes, a prizefighter, and a distinguished fellow physician were among those who passed through the house on rue Lesueur.

So many were disappearing, and so many disappearances were linked to M. Eugène, that the Gestapo arrested him in May 1943—not for killing, but on suspicion of smuggling people out of the country—and subjected him to seven months of torture. The Germans, unaware of the rue Lesueur charnel house, searched Petiot's home and office in the rue Caumartin. Finding nothing and confronted with the doctor's steadfast denials, they released him.

Ernest Coveley was sentenced to seven years in a British jail after committing a rash of robberies in 1989. His weapon was a cucumber, which he wrapped in tinfoil and brandished as a gun. After each crime, Coveley disposed of his weapon by transforming it into a tasty sandwich.

Petiot, thoroughly panicked that his real secret would be discovered, went straight to the rue Lesueur, where he sought to cover up the remains of his victims left in a pit below the garage. Petiot mixed skulls, bones, and flesh with coal in his stove, built a roaring fire, and headed for home. But haste and carelessness were his undoing. The blaze created a thick pall of foul smoke and started a chimney fire. Summoned by concerned neighbors, firemen found the charred body parts and police went looking for Petiot. He fled.

They found him on October 31, 1944, scarcely two months after the liberation of Paris, posing as a Resistance officer. At Petiot's trial, the evidence included scores of his victims' suitcases, stacked high in the courtroom. Doctor Satan was found guilty of murdering those he purported to help. He was hanged on May 25, 1946. □

Displaying boredom, "Doctor Satan" Marcel Petiot leans on the defendant's bench next to his victims' luggage.

Japanese police chemists test the teacups used to poison employees of Tokyo's Teikoku Bank.

Bitter Medicine

Employees of the Shiinamachi branch of the Teikoku Bank expressed no reservations when a man came in on January 26, 1948, and asked them to gulp down a vile-tasting solution. The visitor, who said he was a physician with the Metropolitan Tokyo Health and Sanitation Authority, promised that the distasteful medicine would protect the workers from a spreading dysentery epidemic.

Within minutes of sipping the liquid, ten workers were dead and four others were incapacitated. Only one was later able to describe the visitor. The so-called medicine was deadly potassium cyanide, and the "medical authority" was a bank robber who had devised a clever and ruthless plot. Although the impostor ignored an open safe containing even more money, the robbery netted about $500 in cash.

In post-World War II Japan, that was a substantial sum.

During their investigation, police learned that the Teikoku Bank was apparently the third—and sole successful—target of the mysterious poisoner. Several months earlier, another Tokyo bank had been approached by a man posing as a health official. He administered what he said was an antidote to an epidemic disease, but the poison was apparently too weak to have any serious effects, and the would-be robber left. Only one week before the Teikoku robbery, a man approached yet another bank, telling the manager that he was there to disinfect money tainted by a recent epidemic. But the manager brusquely replied that the workers were too busy, and the "health official" walked out.

Despite these three appearances, clues were in short supply. Detectives questioned more than 5,000 people. They even asked a group of mystery writers to apply their

imagination to the case in the hope that one of the resulting scenarios might yield a promising lead. None did.

At last, on August 21, seven months after the Teikoku murders, police arrested Sadamichi Hirasawa, an artist who had lived near the bank. Hirasawa matched the description that some of the survivors gave of the Teikoku murderer. Moreover, he had recently come into a large sum of money, and he had moved out of his home shortly after the slayings. He also used cyanide in his paints. The evidence was hardly conclusive, but Hirasawa was nevertheless convicted and sentenced to death. He filed several appeals, and the sentence was never imposed. He was never freed, either, however, and Hirasawa achieved the dubious distinction of becoming one of the longest-serving death-row inmates in history, dwelling in Miyagi Prison from July 1950 until his death at age ninety-five in May 1987. □

Speaking Up

The first of the bombs, a piece of brass pipe stuffed with gunpowder that failed to ignite, appeared on November 16, 1940, in a toolbox at the Consolidated Edison plant on West Sixty-Fourth Street in Manhattan. An attached note warned, "Con Ed crooks, this is for you." Consolidated Edison, New York City's huge supplier of electricity and steam, appeared to be the object of someone's anger, for a second unexploded bomb was found ten months later in the street near another Con Ed plant. Although police linked the two devices by their construction, the case was not pursued with any particular vigor; there were other, more dangerous concerns than these amateur efforts. Europe was at war, and the United States seemed likely to follow. Spies and saboteurs were thought to lurk throughout the city.

Three months after the second bomb was found, America had entered World War II—and police learned that the bungling Con Ed bomber had given New York a reprieve: "I will make no more bomb units for the duration of the war," he announced in large block letters printed on a sheet of paper mailed from the suburbs to the New York City police headquarters. But he added a warning: "Later I will bring the Con Edison to justice—they will pay for their dastardly deeds." The note was signed with the mysterious initials F.P.

The author then turned to mailed threats, complaining of more unspecified "dastardly deeds." At least sixteen notes were mailed to Consolidated Edison, newspapers, department stores, and theaters in New York between 1941 and 1946. But the bomber was as good as his word, never planting another explosive until March 29, 1950, when his third was discovered in Grand Central Station. It, too, turned out to be a dud. The next one was not.

On April 24, 1950, a bomb demolished a telephone booth in the public library on Fifth Avenue. Another exploded in Grand Central Station four months later. No injuries resulted. That changed swiftly in 1951 and later years, as bombs went off in subway lockers, phone booths, theaters—including the famed Radio City Music Hall—Macy's and other department stores, Con Ed buildings, the Empire State Building, and again at Grand Central Station.

By 1957, the Mad Bomber—the nickname had been given in 1952—had planted fifty-four homemade bombs. Thirty-seven of them exploded. Miraculously, no one was killed, although twenty-two people were injured and countless more were scared out of their wits. The bomber seemed to strike randomly; although he appeared to have a grudge against Con Edison, his attacks were not restricted to the company. He called newspapers and wrote long, bitter diatribes against those who took advantage of others. And nobody knew what he wanted.

Police certainly tried to find out. Aided by psychiatrists, newspapers, Con Edison, and scores of ordinary citizens, police investigated countless leads. Finally, the effort paid off. Exhaustive examination of employee files turned up the name of one former Consolidated Edison employee, George Metesky, who had complained to the company repeatedly about its poor treatment of him. Quaintly, he accused his employers of "dastardly deeds."

Metesky's specific complaint was that escaping hot gases in the Hell Gate generating plant where he once worked had caused him to contract tuberculosis. Repeated examinations had failed to find anything wrong with him, and he quit Con Ed in 1931. The state had denied him workmen's compensation, leaving Metesky poor in pocket and in spirit, living with two unmarried sisters in a run-down neighborhood of Waterbury, Connecticut. He was twenty-eight years old when he left Con Ed. On January 21, 1957, when police knocked on his door at 17 Fourth Street, Metesky was fifty-four.

In his living room, the Mad Bomber revealed the meaning of his signature F.P.—Fair Play. At Matteawan State Hospital, where he was sent after being judged insane, Metesky said that he had mailed between 800 and 900 letters to Consolidated Edison, New York City's mayor, the police commissioner, and the newspapers, and "never even got a penny postcard back." The bombs were his way of raising his voice; Metesky only wanted to be heard. □

Fatal Blossoming

Despite her beauty and air of mystery, Elizabeth Ann Short *(below)* had a hard and squalid life in Hollywood. But in her gruesome death she achieved the stardom that had eluded her in life. There were even fans, of a sort, who clamored for the privilege of being named as her killer.

Short left home in Medford, Massachusetts, in 1942 at the age of seventeen, arriving in Los Angeles with distinctive features, long wavy hair that was dyed jet black—and hopeless naiveté. Like hundreds of Hollywood hopefuls before her, she worked at odd jobs and waited for the big break that never came. She became a call girl, feeding her hope on promises of screen tests offered by some of her clients. The tests never happened. By 1946, Short was almost broke and had become little more than an ordinary prostitute.

Then, in early January of 1947, her hope seemed to bloom. Short told friends that she was giving up prostitution and her film career fantasy. She was in love, she said; she wanted to get married and settle down to a normal family life. But the new, more modest dream never materialized either.

On January 17, 1947, a woman walking her young child stumbled on the lower half of a young woman's body on a sidewalk in Los Angeles's Crenshaw district. The upper torso was soon found in a nearby empty lot. The dead woman had been slashed repeatedly with a knife, and on one of her thighs were carved the initials B.D. The body was that of twenty-two-year-old Elizabeth Ann Short. The grisliness of the crime, the youth and beauty of the victim, and the initials incised on her leg sent reporters scrambling for the story. Soon Short's brief life was detailed in columns of florid prose. The meaning of the letters B.D. was revealed by the owner of a Long Beach soda fountain Short once patronized. He remembered her well. "Who could forget a beautiful girl like that?" he said. "Always in black. The fellows coming in here called her the Black Dahlia."

At that, so did the American public, and the Black Dahlia ◊

79

murder became a coast-to-coast sensation. The Los Angeles Police Department assigned 250 officers to the case. Authorities questioned more than 400 suspects, but the murder was never solved.

Oddly, there were scores of volunteers, men and women, who freely and falsely confessed to the crime. Thirty-eight people supplied written admissions of guilt. More than 200 others confessed by phone. The would-be killers soon became so numerous that the police stopped counting them. But they could never forget some.

One woman entered the San Diego police station screaming, "Elizabeth Short stole my man, so I killed her and cut her up!" A man

claimed he had done it and later recanted: He confessed because his wife had left him, and he hoped she would get in touch if she saw his picture in the papers.

The police received thousands of false leads. One came from a waitress who called to report overhearing two sinister-looking men in her restaurant discussing the case. "They looked like they had guns under their coats," she said, "and one of them had an apprehensive look and ordered only a half cup of coffee." When the detective learned the name of her restaurant, he thanked the waitress and hung up the phone, growling to a visitor in his office: "That was us! My partner and I ate there today." □

Brink's, which transports cash and securities between businesses and banks, used the terminal to consolidate shipments each evening for delivery on the following day. At times, the building housed enormous sums of cash; although the thieves escaped with more than $2 million, they overlooked more than $1 million, including the entire $880,000 payroll for the General Electric Company's Boston-area employees.

Brink's potential was recognized in 1944 by a crook named Tony Pino. His accomplishments until then had been small, but his ambitions were great. Pino found that security in the Brink's building was so lax that he could enter and leave at will; once he found—and lovingly kissed—the terminal's huge vault. With the help of bar owner Big Joe McGinnis, Pino assembled eleven confederates. Most were simply journeyman thieves, but the group included two skilled getaway drivers and a locksmith.

The job required patience. For a year and a half, the thieves studied the target. They posted round-the-

Brinksmanship

Few robberies in history approach the magnitude and notoriety of the 1950 holdup of a Brink's armored car depot in Boston. Even lawmen expressed admiration for the criminals, for the theft was executed with a precision that results only from superior craftsmanship and painstaking preparation. It

was—almost—the perfect crime.

The target was the block-long North End Terminal of Brink's Inc. near the Boston waterfront.

A newspaper illustration shows ten of the Brink's robbers and their route to the loot-filled vault.

clock watches, carefully logging the arrival and departure of shipments and deducing the times when the cash holdings were at their peak. One by one, they removed and made keys for five locks between the street entrance and the terminal's counting room, where the cash was kept. They learned that activities in the counting room could be observed from the roof of a building across the street. They broke into the offices of the American District Telegraph Company, stole details of the terminal's alarm system, and replaced the file before it was missed. At last, seven gang members were picked to enter the building during the robbery; two others were to stand as lookouts and two as drivers.

Roles assigned, the gang took the show into rehearsal. Twenty times, the crooks took up their assigned places; twenty times, the seven entered the terminal, passed through the five locked doors, and approached the counting room. Twenty times, they retraced their steps. With each run-through, success became more and more likely. Meanwhile, Pino continued to calculate the flow of money in and out of the terminal with an eye toward setting the date.

He chose the night of January 17, 1950, when it seemed likely that a large amount of cash would be on hand. At seven in the evening, the team parked a sturdy truck capable of hauling the heavy loot on Hull Street behind the terminal. On a flashlight signal from the rooftop lookout, the seven inside men, dressed in dark pants, navy-blue pea jackets, and garish orange-and-black Halloween masks, crossed a playground next to the

building and entered the Prince Street door. In a few minutes, they confronted five Brink's guards, threatened them with guns, and gained admittance to the counting room. As three bound the guards, the four others scooped money and securities into heavy canvas bags. Less than a half-hour after they entered the building, the Brink's robbers piled 1,200 pounds of loot into their truck and left.

Although the total take was more than $2 million, they destroyed nearly half, consisting of securities and crisp new bills that could easily be traced and identified. That left $1,218,211.29 in currency and coins to be divided among them.

Not only was the Brink's robbery one of the largest ever committed, but it missed going unpunished by a scant eleven days. One of the conspirators, Joseph "Specs" O'Keefe, had left $90,000 of his share in the safekeeping of another robber while he served time for an unrelated crime. O'Keefe grew to distrust his confederate, however, and eleven days before the expiration of Massachusetts's three-year statute of limitations, he spilled his story to police. It took no time to round up the other robbers. All received lengthy prison sentences, but only a small portion of the loot was ever recovered. □

Hard Candy

Candace "Candy" Weatherby was born poor, but she was not without certain natural assets—looks, nerve, and a gritty determination to get what she wanted. She wanted a lot, and she got it all—and more, and less: polish, glamour, a rich husband, a young lover, and international notoriety as the star of one of America's most sensational murder cases.

From her dreary beginnings in rural Georgia, Candy gleaned the stereotypical attributes of the Southern temptress. She was at once sweet and seductive, accommodating and manipulative. As a young woman, she was honey-blond, honey-coated steel. Her first lurch toward escaping her origins landed her in a bad marriage, which she quickly shed. There ◊

followed brief stints modeling for toothpaste and shoe ads in New York. Then she moved to New Orleans, opened a modeling agency, and met and married Jacques Mossler, an oil-rich Texas millionaire and World War I veteran twenty-five years her senior. That was in 1948.

Mossler indulged his young bride. Candy later reported that her husband gave her $5,700 a month for personal and household expenses. He also provided $5,000 gifts on her birthday, their anniversary, and at Christmas. Candy happily adopted the life of the socialite matron, taking part in every prestigious charity in Houston. For diversion, she and her husband shuttled between their Texas base and homes in Miami and Chicago.

The Mosslers thus passed more than a dozen years in apparent happiness before their sky clouded over. At one o'clock on the morning of June 30, 1964, Candace and her four children left the Mosslers' apartment on Key Biscayne near Miami and began driving aimlessly around town. Eventually, she stopped at a hospital, complaining of a migraine headache. She was treated and sent home, where she arrived at 4:30 a.m. On entering the apartment, she discovered the badly beaten body of her husband.

What might have been simply tragic soon turned scandalous, for rumors surfaced that Candace Mossler, age fifty (she claimed forty-five), had been carrying on a torrid affair with her own nephew, twenty-four-year-old Melvin Lane Powers, the son of Candy's sister. A few days after Jacques Mossler's murder, Mel Powers was arrested at the Houston trailer dealership where he worked. The company had

been financed by Jacques Mossler.

Police claimed Powers had killed Mossler, leaving a telltale bloody palm print at the scene. Candace, too, was charged after detectives found a note in Mossler's handwriting that read, "If Mel and Candace don't kill me first, I'll kill them."

Candy's reaction to her arrest set the tone for what was to follow: "Oh, pooh," she pouted prettily. When she and Mel went on trial early in 1966, she hit the news media in full stride, giving countless interviews and issuing colorful commentary on courtroom events. When some of her love letters to Mel were unearthed, Candy denied that they had any significance, guilelessly claiming, "I write to everyone, 'Darlin' I love you. I want you in my arms.' I say the same thing to my lawyer. It doesn't mean I really love him." Her entrances into court oozed flair and brass, marked by kisses blown to spectators, reporters, and jurors.

In stark contrast to his flamboyant lover, young Powers was stolid and expressionless. The prosecution tried to prove that Candy had asked Powers to kill her husband so she could inherit his fortune and marry her nephew. The defense, led by renowned Texas lawyer Percy Foreman, revealed that Jacques Mossler had had homosexual affairs and speculated that one of these resulted in his death.

The trial consumed more than a month, making it one of the longest criminal trials in Florida history. The jury deliberated for more than sixteen hours before pronouncing Candace Mossler and Powers innocent on March 6, 1966. Predictably, Candy greeted the verdict with unquenchable effusion, rushing to the jurors and kissing

each one of them, sobbing, thanking them on behalf of "my poor little children back home."

Powers later became a Houston real estate magnate. Candy married an electrician named Barnett Garrison, then divorced him in 1975, the same year that she cut three of her "poor little children" out of her will, claiming that "they have not demonstrated the care, love, and affection I deserve as their mother." She died in a Miami hotel on October 26, 1976, at the age of sixty-two. She was buried in Arlington National Cemetery next to the husband she had been accused of killing a dozen years earlier. On official records, Mossler's murder remains unsolved. □

Something Silly

For more than a year, between July of 1976 and August of 1977, a serial killer stalked the lovers' lanes and byways of New York City, shooting thirteen young men and women and spawning terror. Midway through his spree, the unknown gunman cryptically christened himself, in a letter to police, "the Son of Sam."

The name stuck but provided no clue to the murderer's true identity. A task force of fifty-nine officers worked exclusively on the case. The police identified more than 3,000 suspects, but throughout the winter and into the second summer of the killings, they seemed powerless to halt the steadily mounting toll of victims.

Redemption

Convict number 9305 was clerking in the master mechanic's office of the Northern Illinois State Penitentiary in Joliet when he was called to the warden's office and informed that he had been granted parole. He had already served thirty-three years of a life-plus-ninety-nine-year sentence. "Thank the Lord it's all over," he sighed.

When he emerged from prison on March 13, 1958, convict number 9305 was a balding, paunchy, diabetic fifty-three-year-old—a man very different from the cocky, arrogant youth who had entered Joliet nearly thirty-four years earlier after helping to commit "the crime of the century."

Convict number 9305 was Nathan F. Leopold. In Chicago in 1924, at the age of nineteen, Leopold and his friend Richard Loeb had kidnapped fourteen-year-old Bobby Franks to prove that they could commit the perfect crime. Claiming to seek ransom to ensure Bobby's safe return, Leopold and Loeb instead killed the boy. Far from perfect, the crime was badly bungled, and soon both youths were captured, jailed, and put on trial. The case proceeded amid glaring publicity and an air of revenge against the class and privilege that had produced the young criminals. Both boys were highly intelligent children of wealthy families. Their deed was born of arrogance, their certainty that they were superior beings, above the law. Throughout the trial, neither displayed any remorse.

During the proceedings, 3,000 spectators vied for places in the cramped courtroom, where prosecutor Robert E. Rowe sought the ⟡

At one point, frustrated New York Police Inspector Irving Levitan remarked that no conscious effort would lead to the Son of Sam's capture; only "something silly like a traffic ticket will get him."

A week later, on July 31, 1977, the Son of Sam struck in the Bensonhurst section of Brooklyn. His victims were twenty-year-old Stacy Moskowitz and Robert Violante, a couple that had parked on the service road of the Shore Parkway. Moskowitz died of her wounds; Violante survived but was blind.

When Cacilia Davis, a resident of the neighborhood, read about the attacks the next day, she recalled an unusual encounter that she had had the night before, little more than a block from the crime scene. While walking her dog, she passed a man who moved oddly, "like a cat," and appeared to be holding something metallic up his sleeve.

At first Davis was reluctant to call the police; it probably was not important, she reasoned. And she was fearful that the killer might retaliate against her. Eventually, however, she came forward and told her story, recalling as well what seemed like a trivial detail: The only other people she saw on the nearly vacant streets of her neighborhood that evening were police officers who were writing parking tickets. Police had written many parking tickets in Bensonhurst that evening, but only one was issued to a nonresident of the area—a man from Yonkers named David Berkowitz. He had parked his cream-colored Ford Galaxie hardtop next to a fire hydrant.

When arrested, Berkowitz admitted to the murders. The hunt for the Son of Sam was over. □

Famed attorney Clarence Darrow *(left)* saved young killers Nathan Leopold *(far right)* and Richard Loeb *(next to him)* from death sentences in their trial for committing "the crime of the century."

death penalty. "They are as much entitled to mercy as a couple of rattlesnakes, coiled and ready to strike," Rowe asserted.

Leading the defense was the great attorney Clarence Darrow, a steadfast opponent of the death penalty. He could not hope for acquittal. But, trying the case in front of a judge and without a jury, he did manage to save his clients from the electric chair.

Psychiatrists—called alienists in those days—testified for both sides as Darrow sought to walk a legal tightrope; he wanted to establish that circumstances affecting the boys' mental states mitigated the horror of the crime, but he had to stop short of asserting insanity. An insanity plea would have necessitated a jury trial, and Darrow, perhaps the greatest swayer of juries in the history of American law, suspected that even he could not overcome public rancor against his clients.

In the end, he won their lives less on the strength of any testimony than with his impassioned plea against capital punishment. The defendants would hang, Darrow said, only if the judge heeded "the hoarse voice of the mob which says 'Kill.'" To spare them, on the other hand, would be to turn away from past barbarism and toward a future that would see the flowering of humanity's better instincts.

"I am pleading for the future," Darrow said, "I am pleading for a time when hatred and cruelty will not control the hearts of men. When we can learn by reason and judgment and understanding and faith that all life is worth saving, and that mercy is the highest attribute of man."

When Leopold and Loeb were sentenced to serve life in prison, Darrow predicted that they would be ready for parole at the age of fifty. By then, he argued, their personalities would have undergone a dramatic change for the better.

Darrow was at least half-right. Loeb was killed in a prison fight in 1936. But Leopold was indeed transformed. He helped set up a high-school correspondence course for his fellow inmates, reorganized the prison library, and worked diligently in the prison's x-ray and pathology labs. In 1949, Governor Adlai Stevenson reduced Leopold's sentence in recognition of his service as a guinea pig in the testing of new drugs for malaria.

Shortly after his release from prison, the brilliant and well-educated Leopold took a ten-dollar-a-month job as a laboratory technician in a hospital operated by the Church of the Brethren in Puerto Rico. He lived on income from a family trust fund. Leopold married a widow, received a master's degree in social medicine from the University of Puerto Rico, took a job as a public-health worker, and devoted his spare time to raising funds for the Church of the Brethren. He died of a heart ailment in 1971 in San Juan. □

London police were baffled in 1989 by two dozen random attacks in which vegetables were used as deadly weapons. A fifty-six-year-old man was killed with a turnip. A woman was smashed in the face with a potato. And another victim, a jogger, was clobbered with a cabbage.

Victim's Vengeance

To his neighbors in the upscale Washington, D.C., suburb of Great Falls, Virginia, Norman Hamilton was a respectable investor in real estate and the stock market. Hamilton, his wife, Linda, and their three children dressed well, behaved well, and fit well into their prosperous, achievement-oriented community. But the macabre events of one winter night in 1980 demonstrated that Norm Hamilton's achievements clearly set him apart from his neighbors.

On the evening of December 5, Hamilton was hard at work pursuing his real profession: sneak thief. He had broken into the Washington home of a renowned cardiologist, Dr. Michael J. Halberstam, and was quietly searching for valuables when the doctor and his wife returned to their darkened house. Surprised and frightened by the couple's sudden appearance in the foyer, the burglar pulled out a gun and ordered the homeowners to "hit the floor and freeze." The doctor and his wife obeyed, and the thief disappeared. The ensuing silence caused the Halberstams to think that the intruder had left. But as soon as they rose from the floor, shots rang out; Norm Hamilton had not escaped but simply stepped out of sight as he considered his next move. Two bullets slammed into Michael Halberstam's chest.

A surprising series of events followed in rapid succession. The gunman fled from the Halberstams' house. Grievously wounded, the doctor also ran out the door and jumped behind the wheel of his car. His wife leaped into the passenger seat, and the couple roared off in the direction of Sibley Hospital, about a mile from their home. They had gone just a few blocks when Halberstam spied the burglar on the sidewalk. Yelling "There he is!" Halberstam— ◊

A burglary victim *(below)* searches for her belongings among thousands of items discovered in the home of thief Bernard Welch *(right)*.

enraged as well as wounded—swerved in pursuit. He drove over the curb, onto the sidewalk, and into the burglar, striking the thief a glancing blow that sent him spinning.

The doctor continued driving, but weakened by loss of blood, he soon slumped over the wheel, and the car careened into a tree within sight of the hospital. The forty-eight-year-old physician was pronounced dead on arrival.

Although Halberstam's killer suffered only minor cuts and bruises, he fled no further; he was arrested by police responding to the scene of the doctor's automobile crash. The crook carried no identification and refused to divulge his identity, answering repeated police demands only with the cryptic muttered comment, "You're going to be surprised." He was right. A check of the FBI's fingerprint files revealed that Norm Hamilton was none other than one of the nation's most wanted criminals, Bernard Charles Welch, Jr., who had eluded authorities in seven states since escaping from prison in up-state New York in 1974. For four years, until Welch killed Halberstam, police were aware that he was active in the Washington area. They had amassed a huge file of data on Welch's work, but they had not been able to catch him.

Welch's loner work habits rewarded him with a life of luxury. Over the previous five years, he had allegedly stolen an estimated seven million dollars worth of furs, silverware, art, jewels, and rare coins. Although he had been arrested before, Welch always slipped through the net, either by jumping bail or by escaping from prison. Once free, he adopted aliases, took on the coloration of a well-to-do, upright citizen—and continued business as usual.

The take from Welch's burglaries in the Washington area filled fifty-one boxes and was valued at more than three million dollars. At the invitation of police, 4,000 victims of burglaries in the area trooped past the displayed booty in the hope of recovering their valuables.

Welch was convicted of murder and sent to prison for life. □

SCHEMES AND SWINDLES

The confidence game is well named: By adroit manipulation of truth and lies, gullibility, and desire, the con artist wins the trust of his victim. That accomplished, even the most implausible story, it seems, can be accepted, and even the most outrageous demands met without objection. Swindlers adopt many disguises. They have appeared as government officials, patriots, businessmen, heirs to fortunes, scholars, inventors, and supremely clever investors. But all have a common purpose: to proffer, for a price, the impossible dream.

The Game of the Name

Around the turn of the century in America, the name of Andrew Carnegie, the Scottish-born steelmaker and philanthropist, combined the power of both money and celebrity. Invoking Carnegie's name in the right way, as Cassie Chadwick learned, could open many doors—including those guarding some very rich bank vaults.

Chadwick *(right)* was born Betsy Bigley in Canada about 1857. Details of her life are sketchy, but apparently she was most comfortable living by her wits. At the age of twenty-two, she evaded a sentence for forgery by acting insane. Several other brushes with the law stained her next two decades. By 1902, she was living in Cleveland, middle-aged, and married to Dr. Leroy Chadwick, a prominent physician. Now known as Mrs. Cassie Chadwick, the lady found that her wit for fraud was irrepressible and that her standing in local society would enable her to execute an imaginative and lucrative deceit.

She would pose as the illegitimate daughter of Andrew Carnegie, dropping just enough hints of wealth that Cleveland's bankers would be willing to extend unlimited credit. Her own effort was largely confined to concocting the scheme; most of the work was done by the city's social gossip mill. The mixture of scandal, wealth, and celebrity was irresistible. Once Chadwick's supposed paternity was hinted at, it was confirmed and spread by a whispering campaign that quickly reached the ears of nearly all the bankers and financiers she intended to deceive.

Chadwick risked one audacious move to start the campaign rolling. She took a gossipy Cleveland banker to Carnegie's home in New York, supposedly to meet the great man. While the banker sat outside in a taxi, she entered the house, only to reemerge twenty minutes later to say that her father was indisposed. The banker could not know that Chadwick had spent the time talking not to Carnegie, but to his housekeeper. Although the steel baron purportedly had no time for her companion, Chadwick then announced, he had time—and more—for her. Out of her purse she popped a sealed envelope containing five million dollars' worth of securities just given to her. She and the banker returned to Cleveland, and Chadwick relaxed while the fish took her bait, for that was what the envelope represented.

After news of the packet spread, she approached another local banker and asked him to put it in safekeeping for her. Rumor had done its work well. He proved to be so awed by the Carnegie connection that he happily gave her a receipt for the supposed contents without ever checking them.

Now armed with apparent proof that she owned five million dollars' worth of capital, Chadwick went on a borrowing spree of historic proportions. In the next two years, she used the supposed Carnegie connection, plus her own legitimate position in Cleveland society as the wife of a wealthy physician, to amass debts of two million dollars in banks stretching from Cleveland to Boston. She used the money to fill her house with artworks and curios and to host some of the most generous entertainments that Cleveland had ever seen.

But by Easter of 1904, Chadwick was having difficulties maintaining the debt, a feat that required ever more borrowings to keep up the interest payments. At the same time, the supply of bankers willing to lend large sums on a receipt was diminishing. In November, a Boston banker sued to recover $190,000 owed to him and also got a court order to examine the securities Chadwick had offered as collateral. When the envelope was opened, it was found to contain only worthless paper.

With that revelation, Chadwick's credit balloon burst—taking with it several gullible bankers and tens of thousands of innocent depositors in the Wade Park Bank in Boston: The bank failed as a result of her bad debts. Cassie Chadwick was tried in Cleveland on March 6, 1905, and found guilty on nine counts of fraud. Sentenced to ten years' imprisonment, she died two years later in jail.

A quiet, impassive spectator watched in court as she was sentenced: Andrew Carnegie had come to hear the story of the woman who had misused his name. □

Renting Arizona

In 1883, posters began appearing in Phoenix and in other southwestern towns advertising an incredible claim. According to the broadsides, everything within a 17,000-square-mile chunk of southern Arizona and part of New Mexico belonged to one James Addison Reavis, a forty-year-old Missouri-born drifter who had visited the region for the first time just three years before. The posters further announced that Reavis expected all those occupying his land—cities, homesteads, mines, and railways—to register and pay rent.

Reavis said he owned documents that backed up his claim—papers spelling out terms of a huge land grant made 135 years earlier by the king of Spain to a nobleman named Don Miguel de Peralta. The United States had agreed to honor all such land-grant titles under the treaty of 1848 settling the Mexican War. In fact, the claim was entirely spurious. Reavis had heard about the Peralta grant while he was selling newspaper advertising in San Francisco in the late 1870s—the same time that he became aware of the railroads' intense interest in southwestern land. In 1880, he visited Arizona and obtained papers that he said supported the Peralta title. He knew that the documents were worthless, but he was a born forger who had practiced his art faking passes for his fellow Confederate soldiers during the Civil War. Now he had the raw materials for a major coup.

Working feverishly for the next three years, Reavis invented and documented a dynasty of Peraltas and a history of their activities over more than a century. He traveled to Mexico and Spain, where he altered manuscripts in historic libraries so that they would back his claims. He even worked in stone; high up in the Sierra Estrella, southwest of Phoenix, he carved a phony inscription that purported to mark the western boundary of his realm.

Reavis further buttressed his case by creating a female heir to the Peralta line. He found an illit-erate Mexican girl of sixteen and had her expensively educated at a convent. Meanwhile, he created a new dossier of phony documents proving that she was the last living descendant of Don Miguel de Peralta. Reavis married her on December 31, 1882, thereafter styling himself the baron of Arizona.

Reavis's claim was the largest ever presented to the U.S. government, and it languished with the ◊

Photographs of James Addison Reavis and his wife, a Mexican girl billed as the last heir to a fortune in land, appeared in a brochure for investors at the height of his Arizona land scheme in the early 1880s.

U.S. surveyor general for nearly seven years. During that time, many in the affected territory, including railroad companies and mine owners, chose to settle with their presumptive landlord. Their rents permitted Reavis to live the life of a wealthy aristocrat. He traveled throughout Europe—where he modified his title to the baron de Arizonac and arranged meetings with members of the aristocratic Rothschild family and even Queen Victoria of England.

The payments continued even after 1890, when the surveyor gen-eral reported unfavorably on Reavis's claim and cast doubt on the validity of many of the documents. But the report was nonetheless the beginning of the end. Mallet Prevost, a special investigator for the U.S. Court of Private Land Claims, sailed for Spain in 1894 to examine colonial records kept in archives in Seville. He used newly developed photographic techniques and chemical testing of ink and paper to prove that the papers essential to Reavis's case had been tampered with.

Prevost also revealed that Reavis was not as careful as he should have been. To establish his wife's credentials, the claimant had entered her birth in the registry of the California village where she was supposed to have been born. But he failed to also record it in the village priest's private register.

Reavis was brought to trial in 1896 and sentenced to two years' imprisonment. The baron of Arizona eventually returned to California, where he briefly published a magazine about the Peralta grant. He died in 1914 and was buried in a pauper's grave in Denver. □

Leaky Ship

Somerset House in London is the central registry for all wills made in England, and its records go back for centuries. The files are remarkably accessible; they can be consulted by the public for a small fee. But in the 1920s, when transatlantic travel and communications were far more difficult than they are today, London was a long way from Madison County, Iowa. And Oscar Marril Hartzell, a farmer turned con artist, used that fact to extract at least two million dollars from more than 70,000 people in the greatest swindle of his day.

Unlike most successful scams, Hartzell's project did not even have the virtue of originality. The idea, already old when Hartzell came across it, involved the legacy of the sixteenth-century English buccaneer Sir Francis Drake. According to the story, Drake had an affair with Queen Elizabeth, and to prevent this from being revealed in the adventurer's will, the document was never probated. Instead, his estate was confiscated by the queen's ministers. The vast fortune he had gained by seizing Spanish treasure ships therefore awaited his rightful heirs—if only they had the time and the money to fight their claim through the British courts.

The problem was that the story was completely untrue. Drake had in fact filed a will, dated August 13, 1595, and it had been duly probated. In any case, British law specified a statute of limitations in such cases of thirty years. Even if there had been any truth in Hartzell's story, he was three centuries too late to establish a claim. It would take fourteen years for Hartzell's victims to discover the truth, however—a costly delay.

The dupes were all subscribers to the Sir Francis Drake Association, the organization Hartzell created to pursue the fictitious legacy. He set up the society in 1919, claiming to represent Drake's legitimate heirs. At first he targeted people with the surname of Drake, then widened the net by promising a share of the loot to anyone who invested in his scheme. The reward was to be proportionate to the investment made.

Those promised returns were huge, if vaguely stated. Hartzell never specified the exact amount that he expected from Drake's will, but he once indicated that it would be more than enough to buy the state of Iowa and everything in it. Pending this nebulous bonanza, however, Hartzell was able to keep hard cash coming into his own coffers. This was accomplished by a network of twenty-one agents, each responsible for a specific territory—and for sending $2,500 to Hartzell each week. He kept his investors' interest with regular newsletters that detailed the supposed progress of the claim.

Hartzell also took precautions to protect himself. He knew that the main threat of exposure lay with the postal authorities, who could bring charges of mail fraud, so he avoided the mails and conducted all his correspondence by telegram and international cable. In addition, contributors were sworn to secrecy, on the spurious ground that publicity could endanger the delicate negotiations Hartzell was conducting with the British government. For twelve years, he lived in high style in London off funds gleaned from the con.

Hartzell's downfall came, as he had foreseen, through the post office. Although he personally avoided using the mails, his agents were not always so careful. In 1933, seven of them were charged with mail fraud. When the gigantic scale of the operation became apparent, Hartzell himself was deported from England back to the United States to face charges of promoting a scheme to defraud. Found guilty, he was sentenced to ten years' imprisonment.

But that was not the end of the scheme. So many of Hartzell's victims refused to give up their delusions that he was able to continue the scam when he was released on bail pending an appeal. The appeal was denied, and Hartzell was sent to prison. Charged with reopening his scam while on bail, he was tried again in 1936 and convicted. Hartzell ended his days seven years later as a mental patient in the Medical Center for Federal Prisoners at Springfield, Missouri. And even then there remained hopeful investors who continued to treasure their receipts from the Sir Francis Drake Association, hoping that someday, somehow, their ship would come in. □

The Yellow Kid

Everyone always agreed that the Yellow Kid had style. Born Joseph Weil in Chicago in 1877, he took his nickname from a cartoon character of the 1890s and bolstered it with elegant props: He wore yellow dress gloves, carried a yellow calling card, and drove a yellow car.

Proud of his intelligence, Weil (overleaf) made the works of the philosophers Friedrich Nietzsche and Herbert Spencer his bedtime reading. He himself was the subject of another eminent writer, Nobel Prize winner Saul Bellow, who profiled Weil in a 1956 article in the *Reporter* magazine titled "A Talk with the Yellow Kid."

Weil was a peculiar celebrity—a confidence man whose career covered more than four decades, during which he practiced almost every conceivable form of deceit. But he is best known for perfecting the scam known as the Big Store, an elaborate form of confidence trick portrayed in the hit movie *The Sting*. The Big Store involves renting premises and importing a cast of actors to convince the victim that he is in a genuine place of business. Once the money has been handed over, the actors vanish, and so does the cash.

The Yellow Kid's most memorable Big Store is said to have been established around 1910 in Muncie, Indiana. Learning that the local branch of the Merchant National Bank was relocating, Weil arranged to rent the vacant building for a week. When he was done furnishing it, the place looked as though the bank had never moved. Weil even provided genuine Merchant National deposit slips purloined from other branches. A ◊

uniformed streetcar conductor did service at the door as a guard.

The chosen victim's name is lost to history: His shame at being a mark probably prevented his own disclosure of the incident, and Weil, perpetrator of hundreds of scams, probably forgot it. In any case, the man was a wealthy citizen of a neighboring town, and he had been cultivated by Weil for some time. He was invited to Muncie to learn the details of a surefire business venture from the bank's president, played by Weil. If all went well, the mark would buy in for a mere $50,000. When the victim arrived, he was kept waiting for an hour. During that time, customers bustled in and out, and messengers carried in deliveries of money in sacks. The activity was, of course, entirely bogus. All the characters were played by gamblers, petty criminals, and prostitutes of Weil's acquaintance.

By the time the "bank president" was finally free to see him, the victim had no reason to doubt that matters were anything other than they seemed, and he happily handed over his money. By the time he discovered his error, the Yellow Kid was long gone, and that branch of Merchant National had disappeared with him.

Weil often resorted to a less elaborate version of the Big Store, one requiring a double deception. First the con man would introduce himself to a genuine bank manager as a wealthy out-of-town client. He would then ask to borrow the manager's office for a short time to conduct some confidential business. The manager, eager to oblige a potentially valuable customer, would usually agree.

At that, a confederate would bring in the mark, who was persuaded that Weil was running the bank. More than once, the genuine bank official subsequently found himself accused of fraud.

Weil was arrested twenty-five times and served five terms in jail. Along the way, he claimed to have netted eight million dollars. But he wound up with nothing to show for it. Ironically, the Yellow Kid lost his fortune all legally— through real-estate investments that went sour. □

The Pyramid Builder

Unlike the pyramids of Egypt, whose construction required massive amounts of raw material and labor, those of the modern swindler can be erected with little more than a bright idea and a silver tongue. The swindler's pyramid takes its name from the fact that the profits at the top depend on a broad base of hundreds or thousands of small investors. But the analogy is imperfect. The Egyptians built their pyramids from the bottom up, on a firm foundation; the swindler builds without a foundation, instead supporting his structure by constantly shoving new material—that is, new investors— into the layers below him. Eventually, he fails, and the entire structure collapses.

In its early stages, a pyramid scheme seems to possess magical properties. The organizer convinces a few people that he has a surefire success and promises great returns. When he delivers on his promises to the original investors, word of mouth spreads the message that there is money to be made. The first investors are paid off handsomely with cash provided by the new arrivals, and the whispered rumor of profit becomes a shout. Soon strangers are clamoring to give their savings to the supposed financial wizard; and the more money they hope to make, the greater is their disillusionment when someone eventually points out that the pyramid's foundation is nonexistent.

Although such schemes are perhaps as old as the Egyptian pyramids themselves, few scams are as well remembered as the one engineered by Charles Ponzi *(below)*, an Italian immigrant in Boston. Between September 1919 and August 1920, the thirty-five-year-old Ponzi was transformed from a sixteen-dollar-a-week clerk into a multimillionaire. Then he went to jail. His name has become synonymous with pyramid fraud; law officers still refer to such felonies as Ponzi schemes.

Ponzi's idea involved international postal-reply coupons. These are used by overseas buyers of U.S. goods to pay the postage on their purchases. In the course of his job at an import-export company, Ponzi realized that the coupons could be bought abroad for as little as one-fifth of their value in America, because the price was fixed by international treaty.

Ponzi promptly quit his clerking job to set up an investment business based on exploiting the cost differential. He was soon to regret that decision: It turned out that the costs of buying up the coupons and converting them into hard cash made the scheme impractical. But Ponzi also discovered something just as important: The concept *sounded* so plausible that people were ready to invest in it on the idea alone.

Ponzi never bought more than a handful of coupons. Instead, he spread the word of his discovery; and once the money started flowing in, he offered his investors 50 percent interest after only ninety days. He proved himself as good as his word, personally handing over the checks to the beneficiaries. He could afford to be generous: The rush of newcomers eager to join in the bonanza meant that money was flooding in. By the spring of 1920, a quarter of a million dollars was reaching his office every day, and he needed six-teen tellers just to record the funds and take them to the bank.

Ponzi used the money to buy himself a controlling interest in a leading Boston bank, which then became another easy source of ready cash. When newspaper reports suggested that there were not enough international reply coupons in the world to provide collateral for his wealth, he countered by claiming that the postal-coupon business was only camouflage masking the real source of his wealth—which, of course, he had no intention of divulging.

But postal authorities and at least one newspaper, the *Boston Post,* were convinced that Ponzi was a fraud. They learned that his fortune was invested in conventional bank accounts paying a mere 5 percent interest a year—a far cry from the 200 percent annually that he promised investors in his scheme. From Montreal police, postal investigators also learned that, under a different name, Ponzi had served a three-year sentence in Canada for forgery.

Two days after that revelation, on August 13, 1920, Ponzi was under arrest. He pleaded guilty to fraud and was sentenced to five years in jail. Freed from the first jail sentence, he was soon charged with grand larceny, convicted, and jailed again. When he finally emerged from prison in 1934, he was deported to his native Italy.

There he joined Mussolini's Fascist party and was rewarded with a job as business manager for the Italian state airline in Rio de Janeiro. With Mussolini's downfall in 1943, the job vanished. The man who had once conned 40,000 investors out of more than $15 million died a pauper in 1949. □

Lofty Ambitions

As his assumed title proclaims, Count Victor Lustig had greater ambitions than his father, who was the mayor of a small town in Czechoslovakia. In search of fame and fortune, Lustig abandoned his native land shortly after the turn of the century. Shuttling between France and America with wealthy travelers on the era's luxurious ocean liners, he began building a fortune by bilking the rich who idled away their passage at the bridge table. On land, Lustig was a confidence trickster whose most common scam involved the sale of a box that could—according to Lustig—manufacture dollar bills. Just turn the crank and out came real money. Of course, those foolish enough to buy the contraption soon discovered its secret: a small supply of genuine bills concealed within, which ran out soon after Lustig disappeared.

So much for fortune. Lustig achieved fame of a sort in the 1920s by selling Paris's Eiffel Tower to unsuspecting businessmen—not once, but twice.

The idea was hatched when Lustig read a newspaper story about structural problems affecting the Eiffel Tower. An engineer who had inspected the structure said that its defects were so great that unless it was repaired quickly it might have to come down.

Hiring a private suite at the luxurious Hotel Crillon, he sent invitations, printed on forged writing paper of the Post and Telegraph Ministry, to a half-dozen leading scrap-metal dealers. The letters stressed the need for their cooperation in a matter of great importance to the state.

Presenting himself as M. Dante, a senior ministry official, Lustig announced to the assembled merchants that he had astonishing news to reveal. The administration had found that the cost of restoring the Eiffel Tower was prohibitive; the monument would have to come down. He had called the scrap merchants there to bid for the privilege of demolishing the 984-foot tower and salvaging the 7,000 tons of iron it contained.

Because of the controversial nature of the move, he added forcefully, absolute secrecy was essential; the demolition must be presented to the public as a *fait accompli*. To ensure secrecy, all dealings were to be conducted privately through himself at the Hotel Crillon. He asked for sealed bids and in due course chose one submitted by André Poisson, a wealthy dealer from outside Paris, whom Lustig had already selected as his mark. An assistant was dispatched to inform the lucky dealer that he had won the job—and that a down payment was expected in the form of a check, to be made out not to the government but to Lustig under his assumed name. Realizing that this last demand might stretch the credulity of even the most gullible person, Lustig devised his cleverest stroke—and in the process increased his take. At that time, the awarding of contracts in France was frequently attended by a certain amount of palm greasing. So, when Poisson arrived at

A U.S. marshal escorts Victor Lustig *(right)* to prison after his 1935 counterfeiting conviction.

the Crillon to seal the contract, he found the formerly glib and persuasive ministry official now tongue-tied and embarrassed. He was, Lustig explained haltingly, not a wealthy man, and the contract was very large. Understanding the situation immediately and reassured by its familiarity, the dealer hastened to offer a "commission." Lustig humbly agreed to accept—and at the same time pocketed the larger check—amounting to the equivalent of $50,000—for the Eiffel Tower scrap iron.

By the time the dealer finally realized that he had been had, Lustig was far away in Vienna. The victim was too embarrassed to report the matter to the police. Lustig quickly made note of the fact—and returned to Paris three weeks later to sell the Eiffel Tower for a second time to a fresh group of dealers.

Lustig later returned to the United States, where he became a counterfeiter. He was caught and convicted of that crime, however, and died in prison in 1947. □

Most people who purchase antifire sprinkler systems hope that they will never be used. One enterprising contractor absolutely guaranteed it when he installed sprinklers in a California school. Eschewing such fripperies as water pipes, he simply glued sprinkler heads to the school's ceiling. He was convicted of fraud.

Overmatched

In the mid-1920s, Ivar Kreuger appeared to have everything a man could want. One of the world's leading industrialists, he had built his fortune by first dominating the safety-match business in his native Sweden, then turning to the global market. He was staggeringly successful. By 1926, it was estimated that two out of every three matches struck in the world were made in factories controlled by Kreuger. He was known as the Match King.

He had built his breakneck expansion on large credit lines from the world's bankers, and in particular from Wall Street. As long as Kreuger produced results, the financial men were eager to lend. And he did produce. The bottom line was the rock-steady dividend his companies paid out to investors each year.

Kreuger's success prevented bankers and others from questioning his unorthodox business methods, which were legion. In setting

out to build an international business empire, he had quickly run up against the fact that in many countries the manufacture of matches was a government monopoly. He soon found a way around that problem: By offering loans to cash-strapped governments and bribes to greedy officials, he simply persuaded them to hand the monopolies over to him.

The details of many of the deals were obscure. Kreuger was known to operate a bewildering network of holding companies, many of them located in out-of-the-way and comparatively unregulated countries such as Liechtenstein, Panama, Guatemala, Romania, Turkey, and Hungary. But then the Match King had always maintained that discretion was vital in running a business. "Silence, more silence, and still more silence" was his answer when asked for the secret of his financial triumphs.

There was a practical reason for Ivar Kreuger's secretive habits: Much of his success was based on

deceit. While building up the match business in Sweden, he had falsified the accounts of companies under his control to make them seem more profitable than they actually were. He fooled international financiers with fabricated stories of secret deals with foreign governments. The deals could not be scrutinized, Kreuger claimed, for reasons of national security.

The passion for deception extended into the Match King's everyday life. In his office in the palatial Kreuger headquarters in Stockholm, a telephone rested on his desk, connected only to a button below that made it ring. To impress important visitors, Kreuger would use the dummy phone to conduct fictional conversations with leading financiers and heads of state. The ruse also allowed him to get rid of unwanted callers by pretending to be summoned away to urgent meetings.

Built on borrowings that far outstripped earnings, Kreuger's empire could not withstand the ill ◊

wind of the Great Depression of the 1930s. As credit became harder to get, Kreuger was driven to increasingly desperate measures to keep up the facade of solvency.

On one occasion, he entered a bank in Brussels, slapped down a huge bundle of currency for deposit, and claimed it contained 400 million francs. He was given a receipt for that sum. Some hours later, when tellers established that the real amount was only 5 million, Kreuger apologized for the error and returned the false receipt. It had already served his purpose: The receipt was flashed at a rival bank as an inducement to grant Kreuger a large new loan.

Other expedients were far less subtle. He created more than $71 million worth of phony securities by personally forging the signatures of Italian financial officials on counterfeit notes and bonds.

Eventually Kreuger's need for fresh funds became so desperate that he was forced to sell off one of his many subsidiaries, the L. M.

Ericsson telephone company, to the International Telephone and Telegraph Company of New York.

The deal proved to be his undoing. For the first time in years, outside auditors examined the accounts of a Kreuger firm. A discrepancy of seven million dollars quickly came to light. The news burst the bubble of Kreuger's reputation overnight. To redeem the situation temporarily, he managed to wheedle an emergency loan out of the Swedish Reserve Bank, but only at the price of agreeing to open his books for inspection.

Kreuger sailed back from America to Europe knowing that he was a doomed man. In Paris he learned that questions were being asked about the Italian bonds. He went to a gunsmith and bought a revolver. The next day, the Match King was found dead in his apartment, shot through the heart.

The fallout from his suicide created the most complex bankruptcy case in history; it took accountants thirteen years to sort things out. When they were done, the shortfall in Kreuger's accounts exceeded the Swedish national debt. □

Ninety-year-old Bernard Berenson, still among the world's reigning art experts in 1955, admires Antonio Canova's eighteenth-century statue of Pauline Borghese in Rome's Borghese Gallery.

Ivar Kreuger, the Swedish entrepreneur who cornered the world's market for matches with phony finances, whiles the time away on his last, desperate journey from America to Europe in July of 1930 as his empire was collapsing.

Crooked Connoisseur

Few names in the history of art scholarship have been more revered than that of Bernard Berenson, whose opinions and erudition influenced the art world from the early years of the twentieth century until his death in 1959. The son of a poor Lithuanian immigrant, Berenson was a brilliant student who won a private scholarship to Harvard University, then traveled to Europe, where he built an international reputation as a scholar and connoisseur. During his long life, he received the cream of European society at his villa near Florence.

But recent research has revealed another, less estimable side of Berenson. He apparently realized quite early in his career that scholarship alone would not keep him in the style that he enjoyed. Consequently he formed an alliance with a brilliant rogue, Joseph (later Lord) Duveen. The most successful art dealer of his day, Duveen has since become notorious for his dubious sales methods.

In 1912, the two drew up a secret contract, under which Berenson was to get 25 percent of the profits on all Italian works that Duveen sold. In return for his cut, Berenson would lend the weight of his reputation to Duveen, luring rich collectors and guaranteeing the authenticity of dubious works that the dealer wanted to sell.

One such operation involved the sale of a painting to the American financier Jules Bache, who wanted a work by the great sixteenth-century artist Giovanni Bellini. At Duveen's urging, Bache paid $350,000 for—in Berenson's authoritative words—"an exceptionally fine work of the master painted between 1510 and 1512." Bache was unaware that Berenson himself had already attributed the work to a minor Venetian artist named Basaiti or one of his followers.

Despite such chicanery, no hint of scandal tainted Berenson's reputation during his lifetime. The connoisseur died at the age of ninety-four. A decade later, author Colin Simpson gained access to Duveen's papers. After almost twenty years of study, Simpson revealed the two men's business dealings in his book *Artful Partners*.

Curiously, Berenson never appeared to allow his shady business dealings to interfere with his scholarship. Despite the later revelations, his keen eye and the subtlety of his intellect remain unquestioned, and his works on the Italian Renaissance are considered masterful still. □

License to Print Money

Two hurdles confront all would-be counterfeiters at the very start of the enterprise. First, they must muster the skills to produce bills that look and feel like the real thing; second, they must conceal the press and other accouterments of production. In one of the greatest counterfeiting scandals of the twentieth century, an international band of confidence tricksters traversed both obstacles with a single step: It had the money printed by the printing firm that produced the genuine article.

The ingenious scheme was concocted in 1924 by a Portuguese named Artur Virgilio Alves Reis, who used a con man's skills to realize a counterfeiter's dream: He forged a license to print money.

The targets of his deception were the Portuguese government and the venerable British printing firm of Waterlow and Sons, which then was producing genuine Portuguese currency. First, Alves Reis fabricated official-looking papers authorizing the printing of $2.5 million worth of Portuguese escudos, purportedly to bolster the sagging economy of Portugal's African colony of Angola. A collaborator, a glib young Dutch businessman named Karl Marang Ysselveered, presented the papers to Sir William Waterlow, the head of the firm, and persuaded him to accept the job. Marang also got Sir William to agree to imprint the notes with existing serial numbers. The duplicates, he said, would be overprinted in Portugal with the word *ANGOLA* so that they could not circulate in the mother coun-

try. Naturally, he cautioned Waterlow, the entire project was highly confidential; if word of the printing were to get out, Marang claimed, the stability of the Angolan economy might be at risk because of panic over inflation.

Even so, Sir William was sufficiently cautious to write to the governor of the Bank of Portugal, seeking authorization for the deal. But he gave the note to Marang, who promised to deliver it in person. Of course, the letter went instead to Alves Reis, who forged an authorization, and on February 10, 1925, the first batch of 500-escudo notes came off the presses into the hands of Alves Reis.

To manage distribution of the currency—another sticking point for counterfeiters—Alves Reis set up a new bank in Oporto, the Banco da Angola e Metropole. This allowed him to mix the new supply of money with established currency that passed through his institution. The promised overprinting of the word *ANGOLA* was never done, of course, and the illegal bills were indistinguishable from legitimate cash. Even their serial numbers were identical to those of authentic bills—and that, together with the very magnitude of the fraud, caused its undoing.

The sheer number of new 500-escudo notes coming into circulation—some 70,000 of them—began to attract attention. Then, on December 4, 1925, a bank in Oporto discovered four bills with identical serial numbers; police were notified. Already an investigation had begun, and the next day Alves Reis was arrested. In the chaos that followed word of the discovery, there was a run on the banks, and in some cities troops

had to be called out to keep order. The director of the Bank of Portugal was arrested and briefly held for questioning. An entire year's issue of legitimate 500-escudo notes had to be recalled.

The mastermind served a lengthy prison term and died in poverty in 1955. The Portuguese government sued Waterlow and Sons for negligence and eventually won back a substantial part of the money. The eloquent Marang emerged nearly unscathed. Sentenced to eleven months in a Dutch jail, he fled to France, set up a successful manufacturing business, and became a wealthy and respected citizen of Cannes, where he died in 1960. □

Murky Medicine

Industry observers were impressed with the way F. Donald Coster, president of the pharmaceutical manufacturer McKesson & Robbins, steered his company through the Depression. In the darkest days of the 1930s, when other firms were teetering on the edge of failure, McKesson sailed serenely on, always showing a profit.

The linchpin of the corporation's success was its crude-drugs division, Coster's personal brainchild. Crude drugs—the term is now obsolete—were the raw materials used in processing not only drugs, but cosmetics and the myriad other products that pharmaceutical companies make. Whatever operating conditions were like elsewhere, crude drugs relentlessly heaped up earnings. Coster, it seemed, could do no wrong.

In fact, the opposite was true: Wrongdoing had been his specialty for thirty years. To begin with, his name was not really F. Donald Coster but Philip Musica. The eldest son of Italian immigrants, he had made his first fortune in the first decade of the twentieth century when he and his father set up a food-importing enterprise that managed to undercut the competition by using bribery to avoid customs duties.

Police uncovered this scheme and others, and Musica spent the next dozen years in and out of prison. He then adopted the persona of Frank Costa, co-owner of a company producing hair tonics. By this time, Prohibition was in force, and the tonics—which had a high alcohol content—proved popular because liquor could be extracted by running the stuff through a still. Eventually, revenue agents closed down the business, and Costa disappeared.

It was then that Musica found his last and most enduring alias: F. Donald Coster. According to information he provided *Who's Who in America,* Coster was American-born, a Methodist, and a physician, boasting a doctorate from the University of Heidelberg in Germany. Under the protective cover of these qualifications, Coster built up the Girard Chemical Company, again a producer of hair tonics.

The firm prospered, particularly through its relationship with W. W. Smith and Company, an international trading organization that was Girard's biggest customer. Whenever he was asked for details of W. W. Smith, Coster would pro-duce a detailed report from a major credit-rating agency that showed it to be a large international concern with interests stretching from Montreal to Bombay. In fact, the report was a sham, and so was W. W. Smith and Company. Its only property was a one-room Brooklyn office run by Coster's brother. The deals between Girard and Smith were for nonexistent goods, although each was meticulously documented with purchase orders, invoices, itemized inventories, and sales receipts.

The deception was good enough to fool auditors from the respected firm of Price Waterhouse. Coster's paper pile gave the impression of rapidly rising profits at Girard—and uncommon business acumen on the part of Coster himself. He was a businessman to watch, and he made certain that the financial community was watching. Within three years, his prestige was sufficient to raise the money needed to take over the long-established McKesson & Robbins. Now Coster had achieved the respectability associated with a well-known company name and the prospect of explosive growth. For as well as maintaining and expanding the company's existing operations, he added to them the lucrative crude-drugs division.

Like W. W. Smith and Company, which became a major customer of McKesson & Robbins, as it was of Girard, the crude-drugs division was a fiction. The product never existed, but the reams of paperwork it generated showed a consistently rising profit. Auditors, who at the time confined themselves to checking the paper rather than the plant, were impressed.

Coster did nothing to disturb the scene. He lived quietly with his family in an eighteen-room ◊

Adopting the name F. Donald Coster and the guise of a brilliant businessman, Philip Musica *(right)* brought notoriety to the U.S. pharmaceutical giant McKesson & Robbins in the 1930s.

mansion that was not thought extravagant for a man of his station. It was generally accepted that he lived for his work. He entertained rarely and put in long hours at the office. He sustained his deception for more than a decade.

However, Coster never entirely managed to shake off his past. At least one acquaintance from earlier years had to be paid substantial blackmail not to reveal his secret. But Wall Street, and Coster's own colleagues on the McKesson & Robbins board, never doubted him.

The end came with a general economic downturn in 1937, when the board, fearing cash-flow problems, insisted that some of the crude-drug inventory be sold for dollars. Coster, of course, could not comply: This roused suspicion and prompted an audit; when no inventory could be discovered, the entire house of cards came tumbling down. McKesson & Robbins stock was temporarily suspended by the New York Stock Exchange, and an investigation was launched.

Within ten days, the probe revealed Coster's true identity and criminal past, and on the morning of December 16, 1938, with nothing but prison to look forward to, the greatest corporate hoaxer of the century shot and killed himself in the bathroom of his mansion.

McKesson & Robbins fared better. Market confidence returned when it was discovered that the company's core business—the part that was real—had survived Coster's management. Moreover, the company was such an important part of the drug industry's distribution system that other firms helped in its struggle for survival. McKesson & Robbins recovered and prospered. ☐

The Baron's Bad News

As the year 1950 opened, the baron Scipion du Roure de Beruyère was a worried man. At twenty-seven, he felt that he was witnessing the decline of French tradition—perhaps even a new and unwelcome revolution. His wife, Eléonore Patenôtre, the daughter of a former French finance minister, agreed. They had watched the Communist takeover of eastern Europe with dismay. They noted, too, that there were many Communist deputies in the parliament of their own beloved France. The Communists preached against the evils of wealth and aristocracy. Those views were revolutionary in the baron's eyes, for he knew well the lethal lot that befell aristocrats in the French revolution a century and a half earlier.

One of the people to whom he confided his fears was Aimé Gaillard, a fixer from the Côte d'Azur. Gaillard listened sympathetically. It turned out that he had a friend in the border police—an Inspector Alberto—who shared the baron's concerns and was doing something practical about them. Gaillard suggested a meeting.

When they met, Inspector Alberto had an extraordinary tale to tell. He claimed to be engaged in one of the most delicate undercover operations ever undertaken by the French security services. The idea was to smuggle uranium out of Communist East Germany to safety in Spain, whose Fascist ruler, General Francisco Franco, had impeccable anticommunist credentials.

But the plan had encountered a snag, he said. Parliament could not be counted on to provide the necessary funds. An extra $28,000

was needed. Besides serving his country, the individual who put up the money could expect a handsome profit, for in Spain the uranium would fetch $48,000.

The baron considered it his duty to help. That was all well and good, Alberto countered—but first he was required to obtain a security clearance. That could be issued only in Paris, where Lieutenant Colonel Jean Berthier of counterintelligence would interview him.

Berthier questioned the baron at length before professing himself satisfied. The baron donated his $28,000, and that night Gaillard, Alberto, and the colonel delivered a heavy wooden trunk to the baron's Paris apartment. Inside was a sealed lead cask bound with steel straps on which were stamped the words "DANGER! DO NOT OPEN!" It weighed 135 pounds.

The next morning, the baron had the trunk loaded into his car and, with his wife, set off for Spain. But disturbing news reached him en route: Things were going wrong; secrets had been revealed; delivery would have to be delayed. The couple cooled their heels in a hotel near the border for four days until a telegram arrived telling them to abort the mission.

But what to do with the crate full of potentially lethal material? The plotters told the baron to store it temporarily in his Riviera villa. After a nerve-racking all-night journey, the baron and his wife reached home, concealed their booty in a closet, and began a vigil for further instructions. The baron took to wearing an asbestos vest, which he somehow thought would neutralize the radiation.

For several months, conditions remained unfavorable for delivery. Nevertheless, there was more uranium to be bought, and four more crates duly found their way to the villa, at a cost to the baron of $155,000. All the boxes were finally planted in the villa's garden. Now strapped for cash, the patriotic noble handed over his wife's diamond necklace.

More months passed. Then one night, a visitor arrived at the villa. The baron had met him before; he was an Arab whom Alberto had introduced as an arms dealer. Now he revealed his true identity. He was working for the Communists, he told the baron, and would pay more than one million dollars for the uranium he knew to be in the baron's possession.

The baron turned the scoundrel out of his house and promptly called Colonel Berthier.

The officer grilled him minutely on the man's appearance and promised action. Berthier was as good as his word. That evening he and Alberto arrived at the villa and grimly asked the baron to accompany them to make an identification. They drove in silence to a lonely beachfront road. There, hidden behind rushes, lay the Arab's bloodstained body. In fact the killing was a hoax. The blood was artificial; the Arab was acting a part.

Still more time passed, and by the summer of 1952, the baron's resources and resolve were weakening. To meet the recurrent demands on his loyalty, the nobleman had had to empty his bank accounts and sell his villa. Altogether, the young man's wealth had been reduced by about one-third of a million dollars. In order to shore up the aristocrat's sagging morale, a new character was introduced, a General Combaluzier, alleged to be a former chief of French counterintelligence. He dangled a significant reward before the young nobleman: France's Legion of Honor. The general's words of encouragement sowed the

seeds of the scheme's collapse. On New Year's Day, 1953, the baron's name was to appear among those of other recipients of the Legion of Honor. It did not. Suspicions now aroused, the baron called his lawyer. The lawyer called the police. Soon a special squad arrived at the villa, dug up the garden, packed the trunks in a protective van, and hauled them off to France's Atomic Control Center at Châtillon for analysis. The uranium that the nobleman and his wife had so ardently protected from the Soviets' grasp turned out to be nothing but sand and water.

"Inspector Alberto" of the border police had indeed once been a policeman in Nice but had been fired for embezzlement; the supposed Lieutenant Colonel Berthier was a Corsican named Carlicchi who had served six months for theft; and the imposing general was a fellow Corsican, Louis Gagliardoni, with a long prison record.

Carlicchi and Alberto both received four years in jail; Gagliardoni got eighteen months. Gaillard testified against the others and went free. Although neither the law nor the baron could find anything humorous in the scam, the presiding judge could not resist addressing Carlicchi archly as "mon colonel." □

Their uranium swindle exposed, Louis Gagliardoni, Marius Carlicchi, and Raymond Alberto *(standing, left to right)* have one of their many days in court.

Bamboozled in Bayonne

To the unpracticed eye, there was nothing attractive about the huge storage-tank complex at Bayonne, New Jersey, just across the Hudson River from New York City. But Anthony De Angelis, president of the Allied Crude Vegetable Oil Refining Corporation, found a certain utilitarian beauty in the squat, evil-smelling vats and the networks of pipes that linked them. Here was an opportunity for profit on a gigantic scale.

When De Angelis founded Allied Crude in 1955, he already had a checkered career behind him. One of five children of a poor immigrant family, he had risen from poverty in the Bronx to head a New Jersey meat-packing concern. But the company lost its main customer, the U.S. government, over irregularities in deliveries and got into trouble with the Securities and Exchange Commission for understating losses in its accounts. As a result, trading in its stock was suspended and the firm was declared bankrupt.

But the disaster was only a temporary setback for the resilient De Angelis. Noting that the supply of vegetable oil in America was outpacing the demand, he saw a business opportunity in exporting the surplus, so he set up Allied Crude. The new firm prospered. It won the support of major shipping companies by providing them with fresh business, and in return they were happy to loan millions of dollars to help expand the operation. Within four years, Allied Crude was supplying more than three-quarters of all edible oils shipped overseas.

But while the revenues were mounting, the profits were not. De Angelis built the firm by undercutting all competitors with a reckless disregard for his own return. Despite its booming sales, the company soon needed extra cash.

De Angelis sought to raise money through bank loans, offering the oil in his storage tanks as collateral. The banks required no more than warehouse receipts guaranteeing the contents of the tanks. For these, De Angelis could turn to a name that immediately inspired confidence—American Express, the international financial giant whose warehousing subsidiary managed the tank farm where De Angelis stored his oil. Banks and other institutions were only too happy to accept receipts issued by such a reputable firm. What they could not know was that Allied Crude operatives at the Bayonne plant were engaged in a complex scam to hoodwink American Express inspectors as to the true contents of the tanks.

Sometimes oil was piped from tank to tank so that, as the inspectors made their rounds, they ended

Salad-oil tycoon Anthony De Angelis *(above)* went to jail for borrowing money against phony receipts for vegetable oil that he claimed to be storing at a Bayonne, New Jersey, tank farm *(right).*

up measuring the same oil again and again. Even more ingeniously, some tanks were fitted with pipes under the holes through which sampling devices were inserted. The pipes contained oil, which floated atop the water that actually occupied most of the tank.

Not even these stratagems could raise enough capital to meet De Angelis's needs, however, so he soon turned to the more straightforward expedient of simply forging warehouse receipts. But, knowing that such methods were unreliable at best, he sought sudden salvation from his ever-oilier mess by taking the proceeds from his fraud and investing in vegetable oil futures. He was gambling that oil prices would rise. They fell.

With no way to meet its liabilities, Allied Crude collapsed, taking with it the long-established brokerage firm of Ira Haupt & Company, which De Angelis had used to make his investments.

In December of 1963, the salad-oil tycoon was indicted on eighteen charges of fraud and conspiracy. He finally pleaded guilty to four counts and was sentenced to ten years in the federal penitentiary at Lewisburg, Pennsylvania. In his brief reign as salad-oil king of the world, Anthony De Angelis bilked bankers, businesses, and the public out of $219 million. □

Black Art

Among the exhibits at Scotland Yard's famous Black Museum, so named because it contains relics of Britain's most notorious crimes, are a set of printing plates, a hollowed-out kitchen door, and some finely printed American twenty-dollar bills. Taking no chances, the custodians have stamped "Forgery" on the notes to ensure that they never find their way back into circulation. The collection is an enduring memento of a counterfeiting operation that authorities described as the "world headquarters" of forgery.

The phony bills are the creation of master counterfeiter Charles Black, a Londoner who applied great skills as a printer and inventor to the task of fooling the U.S. Treasury and the Bank of England. He sometimes failed—Black spent three spells in prison—but it was never because of the quality of his work. His bills, according to one American Treasury expert, are the finest forgeries ever produced.

Ironically, Black was in jail for passing stolen checks when the bulk of the counterfeiting that he made possible took place. Although his house had been thoroughly searched in September of 1971, at the time of his check-kiting arrest, Black's darkroom and printing operation escaped detection. Police walked past the darkroom, and they missed his negatives, which had been sequestered within a carved-out panel of the kitchen door.

It was a close call for Black and a serious oversight on the part of Scotland Yard. Before his arrest, Black had run off $500,000 worth of twenty-dollar bills. Out on ◊

bail five weeks later, he printed another $500,000 worth.

Finally sent off for a five-year term in February of 1972, Black was able to pass on a going concern to Stanley Le Baigue, a distant relative of his wife. No sooner were the police out of the way than Le Baigue set up the machinery once more and began running off additional twenty-dollar bills, adding up to $10 million.

Black chose to make U.S. money, rather than his native British currency, because he had a ready market for dollars: A West End club owner sold all of Black's output at 14 percent of its face value to representatives of the Mafia.

With prison as an alibi, Black was able to escape charges when his press was finally discovered in July of 1973. But Black once admitted that "the smell of ink never leaves the nostrils," and he set up shop once again four years later. Although he managed to print enough money to pay off his mortgage, buy a new car, and open a pet shop, Black was arrested after being traced through contacts who sold the money.

He was convicted and sentenced to ten years in prison. After his release, he retired to his pet store and opened a second business arranging marriages between English men and Thai women. Having divorced his first wife, Black became one of his own first customers. □

Car Trouble

The year was 1974, and the price of gasoline in the United States had recently quadrupled. Long lines snaked around service stations, as American consumers sought to fill the yawning tanks of their high-powered cars. Energy conservation suddenly became the theme of the day.

Into the breach leaped many manufacturers of fuel-saving devices, including an imposing, energetic, 225-pound woman named Elizabeth Carmichael. She presented the public with an economical three-wheeled car designed to save the nation from Detroit's gas-guzzlers. Her car, the Dale, gave seventy miles per gallon, she said. This was the performance of the future, and the

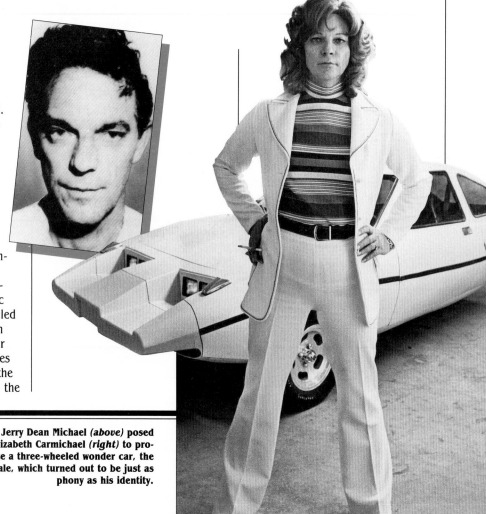

Jerry Dean Michael *(above)* posed as Elizabeth Carmichael *(right)* to promote a three-wheeled wonder car, the Dale, which turned out to be just as phony as his identity.

prototype had looks to match, with sleekly faired headlights and smoothly tapered lines. Carmichael toured the country with the Dale, appearing on television and in person to preach the gospel of energy savings—and to raise money for her company, the Twentieth Century Motor Car Corporation. She raised some six million dollars.

Unfortunately, the Dale was literally the car of the future—certainly not of 1974. It had begun life as an artist's sketch, which Carmichael had then set about turning into reality—or some semblance thereof. From the outside, the car looked elegant; inside, it was patched together with scrap parts whose connective tissue included bent coat hangers and baling wire. The car could move, but just barely; it was powered by an engine of the type used in portable generators and lawn mowers.

The facts of the automobile could not be disguised forever. In September of 1974, auditors from the California Corporation Commission described Carmichael's financial records as "unusual" and ordered her to stop soliciting money from investors.

About that time, it was discovered that Carmichael, too, was not all she seemed to be. She claimed to be a mother of five. The children indeed existed, but in fact she was their father. Carmichael's real name was Jerry Dean Michael, and he was wanted in Florida for skipping bail on a counterfeiting charge. Michael had created the new identity by donning women's clothing and adding the word "car" to his surname. He also added female hormones to his diet in order to look more feminine.

Put on trial in California in 1976, Michael/Carmichael was found guilty of conspiracy, grand theft, and stock fraud. He appealed and lost, but disappeared in 1980 before he could be sentenced.

It took nine more years to track down the Dale's originator. Michael became the subject of the television program "Unsolved Mysteries" in April of 1989, and soon viewers provided tips that led to the town of Dale, Texas, near Austin, where he was living under the name of Katherine Elizabeth Johnson.

The newly captured fugitive claimed to have undergone sex-change surgery. The hormone treatments had indeed provided a woman's bust, but medical examination in prison put the lie to claims of surgery. Thus, when the judge pronounced a two- to twenty-year sentence in 1989, Elizabeth Carmichael, nee Jerry Dean Michael, began serving time in an all-male prison. □

Token Theft

It sometimes takes considerable effort to convert stolen goods into ready cash. But on March 17, 1991, two people made it look easy enough. They parlayed one phone call and a stolen cashier's check into $16,000 in cash and New York City subway tokens.

It is not known how the two came by the check, which was drawn on a New York bank. With the draft in hand, the pair made a telephone call to a token clerk in the subway station at Fourteenth Street and the Avenue of the Americas. The caller, claiming to be a New York Transit Authority supervisor, told the clerk that a couple would soon come to buy a large quantity of tokens and that she should accept the check they would offer in payment.

Presently, a second token clerk joined the first
and ◊

asked to use the telephone. Then the couple arrived and presented their cashier's check for $16,000. The amount exceeded the value of all the tokens in the booth—12,000 of them, worth $13,800 at $1.15 each—and then some. To make up the difference, the clerk dipped into the cash drawer for $2,200. Before handing over the tokens and the cash, the clerk asked her colleague—who was still chatting on the phone—if the check appeared to be valid. He said that it did, and the pair trundled off with the loot. The tokens weighed more than a hundred pounds.

Not only was the check invalid, but the entire transaction was highly irregular. Buyers of large quantities of tokens—and there are many in New York—are normally sent to the Transit Authority's headquarters.

The couple, however, would not have to ride the subway in order to redeem their haul. Subway tokens are regularly discounted for cash at approximately half-price on the streets of New York.

The identity of the token takers remains unknown: They got away with the scam. □

Faded Bloom

To hear David Bloom talk, he was the hottest thing on Wall Street at a time when Wall Street itself was hot. It was the mid-1980s, before the stock market boom went sour with insider-trading scandals and the crash of October 1987. Bloom was only twenty-one years old and fresh out of Duke University, but he boasted of handling the investments of the world's richest man, the sultan of Brunei, and such corporate giants as the Equitable Life Assurance Company and Apple Computers. Bloom also claimed to be a special consultant to the prestigious Goldman, Sachs investment house.

His lifestyle gave his claims credibility. Bloom lived in an expensive condominium in Manhattan decorated with art worth $4.7 million. A chauffeur drove him around town in a Mercedes or an Aston Martin. He ate in New York's best restaurants. For weekends, there was a summer house in East Hampton. He promised a million-dollar donation to his alma mater.

The appearances seemed very convincing to the investors who provided Bloom with the wherewithal to maintain his lifestyle. Most were middle-class people who could ill afford to lose their savings; many were friends of his parents. Although Bloom gave acquaintances the notion that his father was a Wall Street tycoon,

such was not the case; the elder Bloom held an ordinary job in New York's garment district. All Bloom's victims were caught up in the decade's seemingly unstoppable investment juggernaut, and at the time, they were happy to be on board: Each statement Bloom sent out seemed to show that their capital was growing rapidly.

But Bloom's statements and promises were manufactured. He invested the money only in himself, never devising a strategy for coping with the problems that would arise when those who had entrusted their savings to him wanted their money back.

Most never even got the chance to ask, for the scheme unraveled just two years after Bloom's arrival in Manhattan. Business acquaintances grew suspicious of his boasting and learned that his investment firm was not registered with the Securities and Exchange Commission, as required by law. Bloom was charged with fraud, pleaded guilty, and—three years after graduating from college—was sentenced to eight years in prison. □

CRUEL AND UNUSUAL

S ometimes crime pays, and sometimes criminals do—in money, disgrace,
imprisonment, pain, and even death. Hu-
mankind has never been at a loss for techniques to punish its transgressors. Some
methods have been merely bizarre; others, by
any civilized standard, have been remarkably
cruel. Nothing, not even dismemberment or
death by boiling, has been judged too bad for
one kind of miscreant or another.

The course of justice—or at least of law—
tends to be bumpy and
full of odd and capricious me-
anders. Defendants run afoul of cranky
and vengeful juries, stone statues are convicted of murder, animals are burned at the stake
or cut off from the grace of God for their
misdeeds. The innocent may languish in jail
and the guilty go free. The tale of human
jurisprudence was, and is, a tragedy and a
comedy, a balance sheet of brutishness, a
chronicle of quirks.

This four-inch-high fragment of a statue resembling Socrates was unearthed from the ruin above, which may have been the prison in Athens where the philosopher was executed.

Athens's Death Row

When an ancient Athenian was found guilty of a serious crime against the city-state, the citizens of the democratic governing assembly usually levied a heavy fine or the more traumatic punishment of permanent exile. For criminals judged most dangerous, the assembly decreed death and consigned them to the *desmoterion*, Athens's death-row prison.

In 1975, archaeologists studying the ruins of fifth-century-BC Athens identified a building that matched ancient descriptions of the desmoterion. Its suitably stern and unadorned limestone facade had fronted on a busy street. Measuring 40 by 100 feet, the prison had eight cells where the condemned awaited execution. There was also a communal bath and an annex for magistrates and the executioner. His task was a bloodless one. He made an infusion of hemlock, a poisonous herb related to carrots, and measured out a fatal dose for the prisoner to swallow. It produced a gradual, painless paralysis.

In 399 BC, the Athenian assembly voted the death sentence for Socrates, the most famous prisoner ever put to death in the desmoterion. The great philosopher and teacher was found guilty of impiety and corrupting the young—and also, the accounts hint, of being unrepentant and impertinent. Had Socrates disguised his attitude, the assembly might have exiled him or imposed a fine.

During his month-long incarceration, the seventy-year-old convict ignored the pleas of his friends and followers to flee, although, given the prison's lax security, escape would not have been difficult. On the day of his death, with devoted students and friends surrounding him, Socrates drank his fatal bowl of hemlock and drifted into his final sleep.

Among the artifacts unearthed during the ruin's excavation were a number of clay medicine pots that may have once held hemlock. In addition, there was a four-inch-high fragment of a statue of Socrates himself—a perhaps surprising find, since prisons seldom memorialize their inmates. The statuette's presence in the desmoterion may signify Athens's remorse about the fate of the man who was, in the eyes of his disciple Plato, "the wisest and justest and best" of all the men of his time. □

A clay medicine pot similar to these Athenian finds probably held Socrates' fatal dose of hemlock.

Offending Objects

Persian potentates knew how to handle inanimate malefactors, especially watery ones. Around 480 BC, when storm-whipped waves smashed a strategic floating bridge over the mile-wide Hellespont strait between Asia and Europe, the Persian army's march on Greece was interrupted. Its angry leader, King Xerxes, determined to give the strait the whipping of its life. At the monarch's orders, the guilty waters were lashed some 300 times by men chanting, "Oh bitter water, thy lord inflicts this punishment upon thee because thou hast wronged him although in no wise ever harmed by him." For good measure, they also threw in a pair of fetters.

Xerxes may have followed the example set by his predecessor Cyrus the Great during the preceding century. For flooding and drowning one of his sacred white stallions, the wronged monarch tamed the unruly river Gyndes by dividing its flow into 360 channels.

Seeking retribution for the crimes of inanimate objects is by no means a Persian peculiarity. In Greece, land of logic, two eminent contemporaries of Xerxes, the statesman Pericles and the philosopher Protagoras, spent a day together mulling over a hypothetical case: If a person is accidentally speared by a javelin, is it more reasonable to blame the weapon or its thrower?

On the Greek island of Thasos, judges of a similar cast of mind concluded that an object could be held culpable. The landmark case involved a statue that had toppled over on a man and killed him. Found guilty of murder, the criminal statue was cast into the sea, a punishment that gave the bereaved family a degree of comfort.

Among the objects punished in more recent times was a bell in the Russian village of Uglich. It was flogged and sent to Siberia in 1591 for its part in a peasant uprising. In La Rochelle, France, the scofflaw bell in a Protestant chapel was charged with inflaming the hearts of heretics. Roman Catholic churchmen had it taken down, whipped, and buried in 1685.

In England, lifeless miscreants were treated quite humanely under the legal principle of deodand—literally, "to be given to God." If an object was judged to blame for injuring or killing a person—a carriage wheel, for instance, that crushed a pedestrian—it was not fined, burned, slashed, hung, banished, or drowned, as a mortal malefactor might be. Instead, the deodand law required that the guilty wheel be "forfeited to God, that is to the King, God's Lieutenant on earth, to be distributed in works of charity for the appeasing of God's wrath." A major boon to the king's coffers, the deodand law was repealed only in the nineteenth century during Queen Victoria's reign. □

Dog's Life

The Book of Exodus spells out how the ancient Israelites dealt with a badly behaved bovine: "If an ox gore a man or a woman, that they die: then the ox shall be surely stoned, and his flesh shall not be eaten." Nor could beasts, domesticated or wild, get away with murder or even manslaughter in ancient Greece. If the perpetrator was caught, it was slain in public.

Judging and punishing animals as if they possess will, understanding, and the power to reason has its roots in prehistoric magical thinking. Animals were commonly believed to be spiritual kin to people or even ancestor figures—so nearly human that holding them to human standards seemed an appropriate course.

Because of human brutishness, it has often been a dog's life for dogs. In Persia, for example, a dog lost an ear for biting a person or even another animal. And the more creatures he bit, the more body parts he lost, proceeding from head to tail. The citizens of imperial Rome memorialized an event in which their dogs slept through an enemy attack, leaving it to resident geese to sound the alarm. To punish later canine generations for this negligence, Romans held an annual ritual in which bejeweled geese resting on richly cushioned litters and crucified dogs were paraded through the streets.

The records of Europe's lay and ecclesiastical courts constitute a criminal history of the winged, the furry, the feathered, and the multifooted. There was a sensi- ◊

After its errant bell was taken down and scourged, the Temple de la Ville Neuve in France was destroyed.

A crowd of thousands jams the streets of a medieval French town to witness a sow's execution. The condemned animal has been clothed for the occasion.

ble division of labor, with the lay courts handling crimes committed by domestic animals and the ecclesiastical courts specializing in wild creatures.

Rats, weevils, caterpillars, goats, snails, she-asses, snakes, beetles, bears, locusts, mice, worms, turtledoves—all of these creatures and more were cursed and condemned for their part in the vagaries of life. Bees that stung a man to death, decreed the Council of Worms in 864, should be suffocated in their hive, and a seventeenth-century Russian he-goat was exiled to Siberia for butting. Another punishment faced by destructive pests, such as the bloodsuckers that attacked and killed fish in Switzerland's Lake Leman, was excommunication from the Catholic Church.

Before a huge crowd in Basel, Switzerland, a cock was burned at the stake in 1474 for the heinous and unnatural crime of laying an egg. An egg-laying rooster was considered real and thoroughly dangerous because its hatchlings were sometimes basilisks, reptilian monsters possessed of a fatal glance and breath. (Egg-laying roosters and basilisks were, of course, equally mythical.)

Farmers had a good deal more to fear from their swine than their fowl. Some sows devoured small children if given the chance, and the annals of the lay courts are littered with examples of porcine offenders. In one widely publicized 1386 case, a sow was dressed in human attire and executed in front of city hall in Falaise, France, for having bitten a child's face and leg. Similar wounds were inflicted upon the sow, then the hangman did his job. In another swinish

case in 1457, a sow convicted of eating a baby was put to death, but her piglets were pardoned due to their youth and their mother's bad example. As late as 1864, porkers, apparently the pit bulls of their day, paid in full measure for their evil by being burned, buried, hacked into pieces, and fed to the dogs, frequently after having been coerced into producing confessions. Strung up by the hind legs or stretched on the rack, the animals' pitiful cries of pain were taken as admissions of guilt.

Even in the twentieth century, the prudent cat or dog with a taste for forbidden delicacies does well to use stealth in indulging in them; execution of animals is still the law in some places. In the state of Maryland, for instance, any law enforcement officer can kill an unlicensed dog caught gobbling down a game bird. Things go even worse for cats. Merely for stalking a bird or a mammal that enjoys legal protection, a cat becomes fair game for whoever happens to witness the crime. □

A Hanging Tale

It would have been easier and faster for Old West vigilantes to dispatch villains with a bullet in the head. But they favored hanging—an execution method of choice for society's low-down dirty dogs at least since the days of ancient Rome. In the iconography of punishment, the image of a hanged man signals shame and degradation—the fate of vulgar culprits,

the friendless, the penniless, the powerless, the dregs of society.

During the Middle Ages, towns throughout Europe abandoned the handy tree limb in favor of a proper gallows of posts and a beam for the rope. Hilltops were choice spots for the grim structures, which became so ubiquitous that they almost came to seem natural features of the landscape. A common grisly companion was the gibbet, on which the bodies of hanged criminals were strung in chains to rot or be eaten by birds.

The ancient fear and loathing that once surrounded the hanging tree was transferred to the gallows. Decent folk shied away from it in the belief that it absorbed evil forces from criminals put to death on it. Even building one was a repugnant job because it associated the workers with the dishonor of hanging. When a town needed a new gallows, every member of the local builders' guild was compelled to participate so that the guilt and shame would be diluted.

The thoroughly infamous role of hangman was generally reserved for members of the lower class. Serfs, for instance, had customarily carried out the dirty deed for their lords. By the fifteenth century, some English towns had an official hangman, and London appointed its first, a character by the name of Cratwell or Gratnell, in 1534. He had served for four years when he was convicted of robbery and hanged before 20,000 spectators.

Despite their low status, hangmen made good money, and the position was thus sought after. Some hangmen belonged to a guild that tried to maintain, however ineffectually, certain standards. In a well-executed hanging,

the criminal died quickly of a broken neck. All too often, however, death came more slowly by strangulation. If the rope was faulty and broke, the poor criminal had to face death a second time. In a few ghastly cases, the hangman miscalculated the drop needed to kill a man and decapitated him.

However shameful for the victims, hangings were popular public events that drew large, enthusiastic crowds, and the regulars became connoisseurs of the hangman's art. If the executioner did not perform up to snuff, the onlookers let him know it with boos, threats, and ◊

an occasional beating. The most piquant event for these aficionados was the hanging of hangmen, such as Cratwell or a later London hangman, John Price, who swung in 1718 for murder.

On the theory that viewing the consequences of crime was a powerful deterrent, hangings were public in Great Britain until 1868. Whether such spectacles discouraged crime is questionable; arguably, they merely inspired a lust for cruelty. Novelist Charles Dickens attended the sensational double hanging of a husband-and-wife murder team in 1849 and was appalled at the crowd's viciousness: "The conduct of the people was so indescribably frightful," he reported, "that I felt for some time afterwards almost as if I were living in a city of devils." □

Who Was That Masked Man?

"A man lived for long years in the Bastille, masked, and masked he died," wrote a French princess to an English friend in 1711. "Two musketeers were by his side to kill him if he unmasked. He ate and slept in his mask. There must, no doubt, have been some reason for this, as otherwise he was very well treated, well lodged, and given all he wanted. He received Holy Communion in his mask; he was very devout and was perpetually reading. No one has ever been able to find out who he was."

That was the first known reference to the nameless, faceless prisoner whose mysterious plight has tantalized authors and scholars ever since. Despite the good treatment he enjoyed, visitors were forbidden him, and he was to be murdered if he spoke of his past. The mask was probably made of black velvet and not of iron as some storytellers claim. He is said to have died, apparently of natural causes, on November 19, 1703. But, in fact, he had ceased to exist thirty-four years earlier, when he became the man in the mask.

He presents an impenetrable riddle: Why was it necessary to hide his face and identity, but to preserve his life? In 1848, French novelist Alexandre Dumas gave his answer in the popular *The Man in the Iron Mask*, which suggested the prisoner was actually the elder twin of King Louis XIV, locked away to keep him from claiming the throne.

But various other theories flourished. After the French Revolution, some claimed that the prisoner had been Louis XIV himself, jailed by an illegitimate half brother who had taken on Louis' identity and ruled in his stead. This theory had a special contemporary appeal: It claimed that the imprisoned king was the great-grandfather of Napoleon I and thus moved the humbly born emperor into the royal fold. But not even Napoleon's determined search for proof of this claim revealed the true identity of the prisoner.

Oddly, one of the most widely accepted hypotheses is thoroughly sensational: The masked man was the natural father of Louis XIV. Louis XIII and Anne of Austria had produced no children during twenty-two years of icy marriage, but both desperately wanted an heir. When Anne finally gave birth to Louis XIV in 1638, the arrival was heralded as nearly miraculous; the royal couple had lived apart for the previous fourteen years, and Louis XIII was ill and probably impotent. Historians who accept the hypothesis believe that the brilliant and wily Cardinal Richelieu, the power behind the throne, engineered the miracle by selecting a vigorous young man from among the many illegitimate sons of French nobility and arranging for him discreetly to sire the future king. The real father might then have been quietly shipped off to Canada with a pension.

Years later, this story goes, he returned to France, where his striking resemblance to Louis XIV doomed him immediately. No sooner was he back on French soil than the king's agents kidnapped him, concealed his face behind a velvet mask, and hurried the unfortunate man away to a succession of prisons. He was not murdered, the story goes, because even the all-powerful Louis XIV shrank from the crime of patricide. □

The Death of Kings

The mob was assembled at Tower Hill, and Jack Ketch readied the ax. His intended target, the treasonous duke of Monmouth, was already in position at the executioner's block when he voiced a last-minute request. "Prithee let me feel the axe," the condemned man said. "I fear it is not sharp enough." The duke had paid the executioner six guineas to put his instrument into tiptop shape, but the unheeding Ketch hoisted the heavy blade and let it fall. The crowd screamed and gasped. Monmouth turned to stare at Ketch, then determinedly laid his head on the block again to await something more than the flesh wound he had just received.

Monmouth had been right to worry. After striking twice more without achieving the desired end, Ketch threw down his tool and cried, "God damn me, I can do no more! My heart fails me." A sorry attitude for an executioner, and the sheriff of London insisted that Ketch carry on. After two more bootless swings, Ketch unsheathed his knife to finish the job. When the executioner held his mangled prize up for the crowd to see, one eyewitness said, "There was no shouting, but many cried."

Whatever the duke's misgivings about Jack Ketch's abilities, the executioner's alternative method of hanging would have been most unsuitable—and unreliable besides, since Ketch was London's High Hangman. Because the duke was the illegitimate son of King Charles II and therefore at the apex of England's social order, he was literally too good for hanging, which was reserved for lower-class malefactors. Even when it was ineptly severed, the head symbolized the crown—a sign of rank worn only by members of the aristocracy.

From the 1400s until the country's last beheading in 1747, England reserved the practice for its nobility. Other European countries displayed the same fatal snobbishness, and criminals whose rank did not entitle them to beheading pleaded for it as a favor. One fond German father ◊

The duke of Burgundy and his retinue attend a noble beheading outside Paris in 1418.

slated for hanging, for instance, begged for decapitation on the ground that his daughters would be unmarriageable if he died in an ignoble fashion. And in one fifteenth-century spasm of republicanism, the city of Florence granted the royal treatment to common criminals, then reverted to the old class distinction between hanging and beheading.

Democratic decapitation reached its height during the French Revolution, when the guillotine cut across all class lines—Queen Marie Antoinette and King Louis XVI, shopkeepers, politicians, murderous peasants, and royalist priests were equally welcome. Designed by Academy of Surgeons secretary Antoine Louis and named for its chief advocate, Joseph Ignace Guillotin, the device was not, strictly speaking, homegrown, but a refinement of similar devices used in Italy, Germany, and Scotland. Consisting of a weighted blade engineered to fall swiftly between a pair of posts, the guillotine was far superior to an ax in the hands of a Jack Ketch having an off day.

A certain macabre French chic marked the crowds at executions. Women wore earrings in the shape of miniature guillotines, and men dipped snuff from boxes painted with the machine's image. Children played at being executioner with their toy guillotines, which shared the nicknames of the real thing —the Patriotic Shortener, Saint Guillotine, the National Razor, or La Petite Louison, in honor of Antoine Louis.

The National Razor shaved its last customer, murderer Hamida Djandoubi, in 1977. France abolished the death penalty in 1981. □

Collars and Criminals

Well into the twentieth century, Chinese robbers, debtors, gamblers, defamers, and other felons were sentenced to wear a ponderous wooden collar for weeks or months. Assembled around the neck and secured with dowels or pegs, the *jia* weighed from 50 to 200 pounds—the worse the crime, the weightier the punishment. Sitting in a chair was theoretically forbidden, but a bribe could induce a judge to waive the ban.

A constable made sure that the convict never rested for long or took refuge indoors; whatever the weather, he had to remain outdoors. Because he could not reach his mouth, a collared man depended on friends and relatives to feed him. They were allowed to lift the jia a bit to lighten the load on a convict's shoulders, but they dared not remove it. The paper strips pasted near the jia's edges proclaimed the convict's name and felony and served as seals that would tear if anyone tried to remove the jia before the sentence was complete. □

Crimes against sexual mores or marriage, such as rape and adultery, were punishable by impalement in medieval Germany. A rape victim was sometimes offered the opportunity to have a hand in her assailant's execution, starting the stake with three blows of the executioner's mallet. T' official complet' the task.

The legend on this heavy wooden collar proclaims its wearer, Winged Tiger, to be a petty despot, guilty of numerous offenses in southern China.

Nightmare Cruise to Nowhere

When rebellion began to bubble and boil over in the American colonies in 1775, English penal officials were forced to halt the venerable practice of shipping convicts there to serve out their sentences in exile. Conventional prisons were not a quick alternative. Few in number, they were overcrowded even before the colonial uprising. But prisoners and ships seemed to go together naturally, and in 1776, Parliament voted to house convicts in hulks until the American insurrection was put down. The hulks—leaky old troop transports, men-o'-war, and slaving ships riding at anchor in British ports and rivers—would serve as temporary prisons.

Every hulk was a vile, barely habitable place, but the dank, foul atmosphere of the lowest deck was unequaled. New arrivals were quartered there, to work their way upward to less poisonous decks as the occupants above died off, escaped, or completed their sentences. During an economic decline in the 1780s that triggered a crime wave, some hulks became so packed that each prisoner had a strip of sleeping space no wider than eighteen inches. Vermin abounded, and the only fumigation technique was tobacco smoking, which authorities encouraged despite the obvious danger of fire aboard wooden ships. Prisoners itched with lice, which transmitted typhus. Called jail fever because it spread so readily in crowded lockups, the fatal disease swept through the hulks repeatedly.

The government guidelines for feeding prisoners were regularly ignored, and chronic hunger pangs were facts of life on the hulks. Corrupt wardens, cooks, stewards, and crewmen siphoned off much of the bread, meat, and beer intended for their charges, either consuming it themselves or selling it.

Practically speaking, the underfed convicts were slaves. Forced to labor onshore and off for the Crown, they were assigned arduous and dirty work—cleaning sewers and ships, mining coal, dredging river bottoms. The prisoners had literally to watch their step and other minor points of behavior because of the elaborate system of rules. Walking too slowly and not wearing one's hat at the prescribed angle were infractions that could mean a spell locked up in irons, a flogging, or solitary confinement in a fetid "black hole."

The supposedly temporary hulks were phased out only after the colony of Australia became the new dumping ground for convicts in 1787. With the opening of Australia, hulks served less as permanent prisons and more as warehouses for people in transit to the penal colony. The rotten old craft dwindled in number, and the last hulk in England was burned in 1857. □

An English prison hulk lies at anchor in Portsmouth harbor in the 1828 etching shown above. In 1987, New York City acquired a modern version of the hulk, a floating barracks converted to house 196 inmates (right).

Good for What Ails You

After the main act at a public execution in London, when the hangman's rope had done its nasty business and the criminal's limp body had been cut down, a second macabre spectacle occurred. Women mobbed the gallows, snatching at the victim's lifeless hands. The successful competitors passed the cadaverous palm damp with "death sweat" over their own cheeks or breasts or the bodies of their children. The gesture was touted by folklore as a sure cure for scrofula, warts, acne, and other unsightly skin eruptions.

The belief in the curative and magical powers of a criminal's corpse was widespread in Europe and was shared by the rabble and the upper classes alike. A foreign visitor watching an English hanging reported seeing a refined and beautiful young woman, "all pale and trembling, in the arms of the executioner, who submitted to have her bosom uncovered, in the presence of thousands of spectators, and the dead man's hand placed upon it."

Members of the criminal class looking to their dead colleagues for a posthumous leg up in the profession slipped candles into the hands of the executed. The corpse's touch was believed to make the flames of the candles invisible except to the man carrying them, a great asset for the thief plying his trade by night.

A beheading offered added supposed medical benefits in the form of the criminal's blood, said to remedy or prevent gout, epilepsy, and other debilitating complaints.

Unsqueamish go-getters dashed forward with cups, ladles, and kerchiefs to capture a drop or more of the ghastly flow, and one nineteenth-century Berlin executioner did a brisk trade in blood-soaked souvenirs.

Entrepreneurs were eager to acquire criminal corpses, since there was a market for body parts. Especially prized were the alleged lucky thumb and finger bones of thieves. In life they had illicitly palmed more than their share of goods, and in death they were believed to exert a draw on passing capital, keeping the till of a storekeeper or the purse of a dandy full. □

Doing Time Down Under

The destination of the fleet that sailed from England's Portsmouth harbor in the spring of 1787 was an unknown continent halfway around the world. But the ships' passengers were not bold adventurers. They were criminals who had been condemned to serve their sentences in exile in Australia's Botany Bay, a penal colony that was scarcely more than an idea. When the motley vanguard disembarked nine months later and 14,000 miles from home, there was no one to greet them except a party of Aborigines.

Fate had handed the convicts a raw deal. If the American Revolution had fizzled or they had run afoul of the law earlier, they might have been punished by transportation to one of North America's colonies—settled, relatively civilized places whose function was not punishment and whose residents were mainly freemen. Like black slaves, American transportees were auctioned off to farmers and householders in need of unpaid labor. But once the convicts had worked off their sentences—ordinarily seven or fourteen years in length—they were free.

Australia's dragooned pioneers were seldom violent criminals. There were some robbers, swindlers, and forgers, but most had been found guilty of theft. Stealing a bonnet and a dress, five books and a bit of fabric, or a dozen cucumber plants bought one's ticket to the antipodes. Not one murderer or rapist sailed with the first fleet for the simple reason that such offenders were hanged.

Carving out farms was the first order of business, but it went badly in the early days. Few of the convicts were farm boys; most had come off the streets of London and did not know one end of a hoe from the other. Moreover, they were weakened by months of short rations and inactivity, and the farming methods and crops of England were unsuited to the tropical climate of Botany Bay. The heat and humidity rotted seeds in the ground, and famine was a chronic threat.

The prisoners' keepers were just as hard on the convicts as nature was. Dragged down by the weight of their chains, gangs of prisoners labored ten hours at a stretch, day after day, hacking roads through the bush and carving out harbors. At night, the gangs were crammed into shacks too small for everyone to lie down at once. Special punishments—wearing a spiked iron collar, for instance—made prisoners rue their misbehavior. A fortunate few upper-class convicts kept their hands soft and were allowed what amounted to probation because, as one of their defenders explained, "they were unused to active employment."

The penal camps of the island of Tasmania off Australia's southwestern coast were a convict's worst nightmare. Tasmanian guards and officials were known for their cruel enforcement of rules. Prisoners were routinely flogged with the cat-o'-nine-tails or, stripped naked and in chains, left to the tender mercies of a tropical sun beating down on barren rock.

In response to the manifold cruelties of Tasmania, despairing inmates invented a literally murderous game of chance. The players drew lots for the roles each would play: murderer, victim, witnesses. Who won the game is hard to say. The victim lost his life, but he was free of penal horrors. Since no court sat on Tasmania, the murderer and the witnesses enjoyed a trip to the mainland for the trial. After their respite, the witnesses had to go back to the hellish island. Like his victim, the murderer effected an escape of sorts, at the end of the hangman's rope. ◊

A bucolic 1796 view of the fledgling Australian penal colony belies the miserable conditions its inmates suffered.

A modicum of mercy was extended to female convicts, who were consequently less likely to sport spiked collars or shuffle about in chains. Nevertheless, they were, in the terse words of one observer, "treated like dogs and worked like horses." In the early years, most debarking female transportees were barged upriver from Botany Bay to the miserable hamlet of Parramatta. There they were put to work in Australia's first female factory in the jail's leaky, stinking garret. The women carded and spun wool from the colony's sheep farms, then wove it into a coarse cloth named for its place of origin. Refractory workers were beaten, had their heads shaved, or were treated to a punishing spell on the treadwheel *(opposite page),* which produced, by one account, "a very horrible pain in the loins."

Living conditions were appalling. There was sleeping space in the factory for a third of the women. The unlucky excess had to lodge with local free settlers, who generally charged extortionate rents. The government felt no obligation to pay, so a woman typically sold her only asset—her body—to foot the monthly housing bill.

Most men in New South Wales shared the opinion of British marine Ralph Clark, who wrote in his journal that the foul-mouthed "damned bitches of convict women" were "ten thousand times worse than the men Convicts." Nevertheless, when an unattached male—a former convict who had completed his sentence or a free settler—decided that he needed a woman around the house, he went to a female factory to find one. Little time was wasted on the niceties of courtship. The women were assembled for the suitor's inspection, and if one caught his fancy he carried her away a free woman. He was not obliged to make her an honest one, however. Many Australians practiced "colonial marriage," an informal relationship unblessed by church or state.

Often enough, the new situation was hardly better than factory slavery, and liberated women took matters into their own hands. After spending a few days with a man, reported one cynical convict, the typical factory bride "will make some excuse which a woman is never at a loss for, to come down to Sydney; she will get what money she can of him (the Old Fool!) but she don't return again." □

Execution by Elephant

Indian elephants were once the world's biggest and strongest executioners. Bound hand and foot, a condemned criminal was tied by a length of rope to the hind leg of one of the gigantic pachyderms. At its keeper's urging, the animal trotted at a brisk clip through town streets as its human burden tumbled and bounced in its wake.

If the punishing ride did not kill the criminal, he was taken to the place of execution and laid out on the ground with his head on a stone. The elephant stepped on his head, crushing it, a nineteenth-century journalist noted, "as easily as a Nasmyth hammer would a Barcelona nut."

Deemed barbaric by the British colonial rulers of India, executions by elephant were discouraged, and eventually they were abandoned. □

The December 4, 1875, issue of the London journal *Illustrated Sporting and Dramatic News* featured an Indian method of execution.

Wheel of Misfortune

When his overseer at the Stockport, England, jail assigned him the task of breaking rocks, a seventy-two-year-old convict with a bad knee balked. For his recalcitrance, a pitiless judge condemned him to two weeks of daily climbing on Sir William Cubitt's treadwheel—an agonizing punishment for an ailing knee.

Cubitt was a famous engineer whose design answered the requirements of Parliament's 1779 Penitentiary Act, or Hard Labour Bill, with disquieting brilliance. A mandate for forced labor in prisons, it called for work of the "hardest and most servile kind in which drudgery is chiefly required." Unproductive exertion was perfectly acceptable, since the chief purpose of the act was punishment, and prison officials complied enthusiastically. The last prison treadwheel slowed to a halt only on the eve of World War I.

Because it had potential for double duty, Sir William's treadwheel was soon a stock item all over the nation. It punished and had a practical side as well; it could convert human muscle power into mechanical power for gristmills and water pumps. Typically six feet in diameter and twenty feet long, it looked like the paddle wheel of a steamboat, with twenty-four stepping boards running lengthwise around its circumference. The shaft on which the wheel turned had a speed-regulating mechanism that kept its revolutions to four to six per minute.

To turn the wheel, a line of men stood in a row on the stepping boards and, grasping handrails to steady themselves, climbed for eight to twelve monotonous and excruciating hours a day, with only a few brief rest breaks. It was like walking up a down escalator that never stops.

To keep things ginning along, prisoners were required to climb the equivalent of 5,000 to 14,000 vertical feet daily, a regimen that could enfeeble weaker inmates for life. Nor were women spared the treadwheel. In one Middlesex jail in 1824, a pregnant prisoner miscarried after her first day on the contraption.

Besides endorsing the treadwheel, British penal officials devised even crueler make-work. Imprisoned from 1895 to 1897 for gross indecency, British man of letters Oscar Wilde did his turn on the treadwheel and was also forced to join in the "dusty drill." For this absurd exercise, men formed a square, spacing themselves three yards apart. Then, to instructions shouted by their guards, each man bent and hefted a twenty-four-pound cannonball and lugged it to the spot just vacated by his similarly burdened neighbor.

Most detested of the make-work punishments was the crank, a heavy drum whose handle inmates were required to turn a given number of times. Cheating was impossible because the crank had a counter that kept track of the revolutions. On a typical day, a convict turned the handle 14,400 times—1,800 to earn breakfast, 4,500 for lunch, 5,400 for dinner, and another 2,700 to round out the daily quota. When fifteen-year-old Edward Andrews could not meet his quota, the already hungry boy was thrown into solitary confinement and put on a starvation diet. He hanged himself, cutting short his three-month sentence for stealing a piece of meat. □

Befitting the Crime

Pictured on these pages are a few methods of punishment that once made miscreants regret, if not repent, their crimes and misdemeanors. Some of the devices put to penal use were designed not so much to wound but to shame and humiliate. Applied in public for minor offenses, they inspired the sneers and jeers of spectators and at worst inflicted mild physical discomfort. At the other end of the spectrum are torturous practices that maimed and killed—cruel and, unfortunately, at one time all too usual. □

PRINCIPALLY an accouterment for erring German women from the fifteenth century onward, the three-hole neck violin *(below, right)* was fastened around the wearer's neck and wrists. The double neck violin *(below, left)* was designed for women who quarreled in public. Like belligerent Siamese twins, they were confined face to face until they worked out their problem and agreed to stop disturbing the peace.

SKEFFINGTON'S GYVES *(above)* looks like an innocuous piece of fireside equipment, but the iron device tortured information and confessions from prisoners in the Tower of London. Bizarrely nicknamed the Scavenger's Daughter, the instrument was invented by Leonard Skeffington, an official of the Tower during Henry VIII's reign. Fastened around the head, ankles, and wrists, the gyves locked the body in a fetal position. The excruciating pain produced by prolonged immobilization broke down the victim's resolve to remain silent.

LOOKING PROPERLY foolish in the woodcut above, a drunkard wears a punishment nicely tailored to his crime: a barrel that might once have held wine or beer. Traditional in Germany and English-speaking countries into the nineteenth century, the so-called drunkard's cloak was worn in public, to the vast amusement of the populace. One onlooker remarked that a drunk serving his sentence looked for all the world like a half-hatched chicken.

A SHAME FLUTE *(above)* dangling from a German musician's neck mocked his professional abilities. A soundless facsimile of the real thing, the flute had a long clamp that locked the fingers in playing position while the inept tootler made apologies to the muse of music.

THREE PETTY wrongdoers take their licks in the square in Rothenberg, Germany, while passersby enjoy the group's embarrassment (*left*). The man has been locked in the stocks for the offense of laziness, and the two women wear "shame masks" traditional for gossips. The one at left also has a so-called slander stone—actually a block of wood—hung around her neck. Proclaimed as a "house dragon," or shrew, by the sign she wears, the woman at center is also burdened with a wooden ruff as punishment for violating the town's clothing regulations.

IN A SEVENTEENTH-CENTURY woodcut (*right*), a ducking stool bears its occupant downward for a dip in an English stream. Chief candidates for a few moments of corrective submersion were female scolds, although bakers who shortweighted their customers, slanderers, and contentious married couples were also ducked from time to time. The number of dunkings depended on how serious the offense was judged to be. Before being phased out in the nineteenth century, the ducking stool was a standard punishment on both sides of the Atlantic.

THE TRIPLE agony of hanging, drawing, and quartering nears its end for Huguenot Jean de Poltrot *(above)*, condemned for assassinating Catholic leader François, duke of Guise, in 1563 during France's religious wars. Usually reserved for traitors, the punishment began on the gallows. There the hangman took care that the noose choke but not kill, lest the agony end too soon. After the hanging, the victim was disemboweled, or drawn. Finally, each of the traitor's limbs was tied to a horse. Whipped by assistant executioners, the horses pulled in four directions, drawing the traitor taut. With the help of a few judicious sword cuts at the joints, the animals pulled the body to pieces. The remains were put on public display to proclaim the high price of crime.

EQUIPPED WITH a slender tongue plate, a bridlelike iron brank restrains a woman's offending tongue as she is paraded around town *(left)*. The honors were ordinarily done by an official, but a plaintiff husband was occasionally allowed to take over. Widely used for female scolds on the Continent and in England well into the nineteenth century, the brank made a prudent woman watch her tongue. All too frequently, the plate bore brutal embellishments such as razor-sharp edges or spikes that bloodied the tongue unless it remained immobile. Since a typical sentence lasted some four or five hours, avoiding injury was extremely difficult.

HIDING A criminal past was impossible once a malefactor was branded. The German branding irons below include a miniature gallows at far right, indicating the criminal's next offense should be punished by hanging. The letter *F* may signify the city where the crime took place—perhaps Frankfurt. In England and its American colonies, letters on branding irons were for crimes: *B* for blasphemy, *SS* for stirring up sedition, *H* for heresy or hog stealing, and so on.

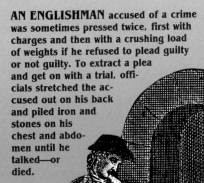

AN ENGLISHMAN accused of a crime was sometimes pressed twice, first with charges and then with a crushing load of weights if he refused to plead guilty or not guilty. To extract a plea and get on with a trial, officials stretched the accused out on his back and piled iron and stones on his chest and abdomen until he talked—or died.

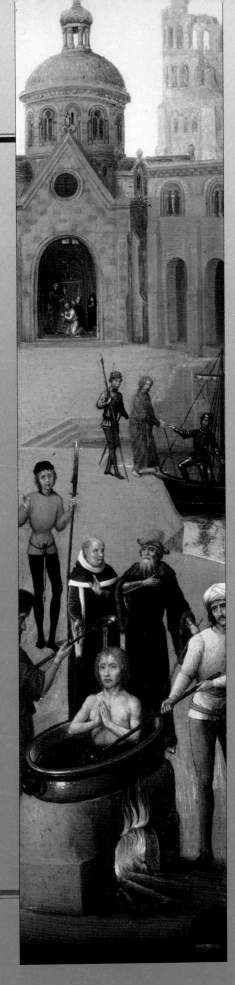

CONDEMNED BY Roman emperor Domitian to be boiled in oil, St. John miraculously survived, as shown at right in a 1497 work by Flemish painter Hans Memling. In later centuries, the gruesome death was dished out to murderous cooks who served up poison-laced meals. English annals note several culinary attacks, including a flavoring of hemlock and other herbs that Richard Roose fed to his master's household in 1531. Spectators in Smithfield watched Roose suffer for two hours in a huge cauldron suspended from a tripod over a log fire before at last perishing. Horrible as it was, the execution apparently was not much of a deterrent. Servant Margaret Davy of Smithfield tried to get away with the same crime eleven years later, and she too was boiled.

Old Sparky

The industrial war of the 1880s that pitted proponents of alternating electrical current against their rivals favoring direct current had an unintended spin-off—a new mode of execution. America was on the verge of electrification, and local governments were weighing which of the rival technologies to choose. Proponents of direct current hit upon a cruel tactic to discredit alternating current. Claiming that it was much too dangerous for household use, they staged public demonstrations in which animals were electrocuted with AC. The animals died quickly—usually within ten seconds—and their bodies showed few if any external signs of injury.

Some anonymous person in New York sat up and took notice. There had been a recent outcry about several badly bungled hangings in the state, and the animal demonstrations suggested a thoroughly modern means of execution that seemed fast, neat, and more humane than hanging. In 1888, New York became the first state to adopt electrocution, and chief hangman Edward Davis improvised a chair to dispatch criminals.

Thomas Edison, an opponent of capital punishment and the leader of the losing DC side, snidely suggested calling the process Westinghousing in honor of AC competitor George Westinghouse.

The first execution carried out in Davis's chair was at Auburn Prison in 1890. The initial jolt of electricity failed to kill the condemned man, murderer

William Kemmler. When Westinghouse heard about the incident, he was appalled. "They could have done better with an axe," he said.

Death often—but not always—came faster and more easily as electric chairs grew more sophisticated. Robert G. Elliot, a successor of Edward Davis, reported that the 387 people he executed all lost consciousness the instant after he pulled the switch. Nevertheless, witnesses recorded disquieting delays and physical effects even when Old Sparky, as the chair was dubbed, was in good operating condition. One convict, for instance, survived more than fifteen minutes of current before dying. And there were multiple signs of the injuries electricity inflicted on the body, including a wispy column of smoke rising from the points where electric wires touched the scalp.

Few prisoners sentenced to death suffered a fate worse than Willie Francis, who was convicted of murder in Louisiana. The state first attempted to execute him in 1946, following its usual procedure of trucking a portable electric chair, a generator, and other equipment from the penitentiary at Angola to the parish where the execution was to take place. On the third of May the big wooden chair was set up in St. Martinville by an Angola guard and an inmate who, though not an electrician himself, worked as an assistant to U. J. Esnault, the penitentiary's chief electrician. Esnault had checked the equipment two days before the execution date, but things went badly at St. Martinville: The chair failed to deliver a fatal current. The electricity stunned Francis and left him

breathless, but he remembered vividly the torturous stabbing pain of the ordeal and the blue, pink, and green speckles that danced before his eyes as the current surged through his body.

A year later, after the U.S. Supreme Court had ruled that a second execution attempt would not violate his constitutional rights,

Willie Francis was electrocuted.

Old Sparky has taken a certain toll on some people on the right side of the law. One-time New York executioner John Hulbert retired in 1926 after electrocuting 140 criminals, explaining, "I got tired of killing people." Three years later, Hulbert took out a revolver and killed himself. □

Mistaken Identity

If a certain London street lamp had only been out of order, Adolf Beck's life might not have taken such a dreadful turn that dusky fall evening in 1896. As he strolled through the lamp's bright beam, another pedestrian stared at his face, then grabbed his well-tailored arm and loudly accused him of stealing her watches and rings. The startled Beck hailed a passing constable, and at the lawman's request, he and his assailant went to the local station to tell their conflicting stories.

Beck had, Ottilie Meissonier claimed, guilefully insinuated himself into her confidence two weeks earlier. In what appeared to be an honest mistake, he had tipped his hat to her on the street and addressed her as Lady Everton. Flattered to be mistaken for a noblewoman, she fell into conversa-

tion with the attractive and elegantly dressed stranger, who introduced himself as Lord Wilton. He asked if they might meet again, and the next day he called on his new acquaintance to invite her to go on a Mediterranean cruise with him. She accepted both the invitation and a large check with which to buy ◊

Adolf Beck, shown at right in a 1902 photograph, served five years for crimes committed by look-alike William Thomas, alias John Smith (above).

suitably fashionable clothes. Noting that her jewelry would not do, he offered to have the stones reset. The foolish Meissonier agreed and handed over her modest collection of ornaments. The check for the clothes proved bogus, and she waited in vain for Lord Wilton to come calling again.

The London police had received virtually identical complaints from other women, ten of whom picked Beck out of a lineup. Despite his claim of innocence, he was charged with fraud. The trial went badly for him from the outset, as Ottilie Meissonier and her fellow victims testified to his caddish behavior. Equally damning were the statements of two policemen who had worked on a similar case years earlier. They declared that Beck was actually the felon John Smith up to his old tricks. In 1877, Smith had been convicted of playing the same con game.

The judge trying Beck had also worked on the earlier case, and he agreed that the accused was none other than Smith. The judge thus denied Beck's attorney permission to enter evidence showing that the accused had been working in South America in the 1870s while John Smith was busy defrauding a bevy of gullible women. There were as yet no scientific techniques such as fingerprinting to establish identity, so the trial boiled down to Beck's word against that of more than a dozen witnesses, not to mention the bias of the trial judge. Convicted and sentenced to seven years at hard labor, Beck was assigned the old prison number of John Smith.

Beck—or Smith, according to the government—had served two years when a staff member at the prison hospital found an odd discrepancy: John Smith's old records stated that he had been circumcised, but the present prisoner was intact. The fact cried out for investigation, but officials dealt with the bothersome evidence with a bit of bureaucratic sleight of hand. They simply gave Beck a new number and sent him back to his cell.

Paroled in 1901, Beck enjoyed three years of freedom. Then, in a grotesque rerun of his encounter with Ottilie Meissonier, a strange woman accosted him on a London street with the accusation that he was the trickster who had done her out of her jewelry. Once again tried and found guilty, Beck was in jail awaiting sentencing for a second time when newspapers reported how a smooth-talking gentleman had swindled two actresses out of their jewelry. Just such a man turned up in a London pawnshop with a small cache of rings, and the alert owner sent his clerk to fetch the police.

The man they caught red-handed was John Smith. A proper investigation proved that Beck was, as he had claimed all along, innocent: Smith was a different person, and he had committed every crime of which Beck had been convicted. The two men were by no means doubles, but both sported mustaches and were similar enough in facial features, height, and build to account for the numerous misidentifications.

The British government pardoned Adolf Beck and awarded him 5,000 pounds to compensate for his years of wrongful imprisonment. But he spent it hand over fist and in less than two years was bankrupt. The embittered Beck died a pauper's death in 1909. □

In 1991, a sixty-nine-year-old Faye Copeland of Mooresville, Missouri, set an unenviable American record by becoming the nation's oldest woman to be consigned to death row. She was sentenced for helping her husband, Ray, kill five drifters whom they employed to help out with the chores around their farm.

Hell in the Salvations

One of the convicts had a good eye—he was, after all, an artist of sorts—and he was able later to give an evocative account of the scene: "Three rounded peaks soaring out of the ocean, the brilliant, almost waxy green of jungle foliage pierced by the shimmering light of white walls, the glare softened by rust-colored rooftops, the entire scene bathed in bright sunlight and hugged between the dark-blue of water and the lighter tint of a cloudless sky." Thus did the art counterfeiter and forger Francis Lagrange describe his initial sight of Royale, St. Joseph—and Devil's Island.

The three sun-washed islands rise from the turquoise of the Caribbean Sea. They are called the

Salvation Islands by mainlanders because sea breezes thin the clouds of insects there and once lessened the risk of mosquito-borne malaria and yellow fever a little. Endowed by nature with beauty, the Salvations were endowed by humans with horror. Far from being paradise, the islands were once three earthly hells at the service of French justice. Between 1852 and 1938, France condemned rapists, murderers, child molesters, traitors, and incorrigible robbers and burglars to hard labor in the penal camps of colonial Guiana. The worst of them—the outcasts of the outcasts—went to the Salvations. Devil's Island, some ten miles offshore, lent its apt name to the entire system. Some people say the name is innocent enough, deriving from the black devil birds that flock there to feed on palm-tree blossoms.

Despite the sea breezes, the environment of the Salvations was thoroughly noxious: Infectious diseases, heat and humidity, snakebite, parasites, anemia, malnutrition, grueling work, suicide, their fellow criminals, and their human keepers killed the convicts off at a staggering rate. Fewer than a quarter of them lived long enough to complete their sentences.

Devil's Island proper was the smallest and least accessible of the three Salvations, with peculiarly swift and turbulent currents roiling its waters. Originally a leper colony, it became the dumping ground for political prisoners. Often no guards were on duty,

for an escape attempt was tantamount to suicide: The would-be escapee would drown in the racing tides or be attacked by sharks cruising for fish and larger prey. On one occasion, a cable strung between Royale and Devil's Island for delivering supplies broke, and guards forced a convict named Saviory into the water at gunpoint to fetch it. His shark-bitten remains were cast up on the rocky shore the following day. The guards routinely encouraged the finny patrol by throwing it the bodies of dead prisoners.

Compared to the dozen or so held on Devil's Island at any one time, Royale bustled with some 700 prisoners. They slaved in the jungles felling trees and quarrying rock. They also farmed, constantly fighting the luxurious vegetation that threatened to swallow up a man's work overnight. Guards snapped a ball and chain around any troublemaker's ankle, and odd couples bound together by chains perforce labored at the same tasks.

A constant threat hung over the prisoners and helped keep them toeing the line on Royale—the 400

solitary cells of St. Joseph, the island of pure and unadulterated punishment. Laid out in rows and measuring only five by seven feet, some cells had no opening except a door, and a man was plunged into perpetual darkness. The rest of the cells had grillwork roofs that exposed inmates to drenching downpours, insects, snakes, and the baking sun. Silence was strictly enforced, but not even the roughest guard could keep men who had gone insane in solitary quiet. And many went insane.

No prisoner knew St. Joseph better than Paul Roussenq, who set the record for time spent in solitary confinement and earned the unenviable title King of the Dark Cell. Convicted of vagrancy in his teens, Roussenq was sentenced to join the French army. A washout as a soldier, he wound up in a military prison where, in a fit of depression, he set his mattress on fire. For destroying five dollars' worth of military property, a court condemned him to twenty years at hard labor and shipped him off to Guiana. He was soon off for his first stint in one of St. Joseph's ◊

The Pittance, by Devil's Island inmate Francis Lagrange, shows a man in solitary confinement handing his food bowl to a guard.

black holes. Altogether, he spent 3,779 days of his sentence in solitary confinement—thirty days at a time, sixty, sometimes more. A diet of bread and water shrank the six-foot Roussenq to 100 pounds of skin and bones. His record is a litany of affronts to authority—tearing up his uniform, trying to talk to other prisoners in solitary, fighting with guards trying to put on or take off his irons, insulting guards and accusing them of theft.

According to the defiant Roussenq's records, he shouted at his guards, "Another punishment if you please!" and was rewarded with another thirty days in a dark cell.

During his repeated stays in confinement, Roussenq scratched messages on the walls—one read "Roussenq spits on humanity"—and worked at his epic poem *Hell*. One verse reads: I am no longer a man/For prison has entered into me/And I am the prison. □

times too smart for their own good, many inmates of Alcatraz dreamed and plotted ways out so often that wardens were kept busy investigating the escape rumors that percolated up from the cellblocks.

To get out of the prison and across more than a mile of swift and frigid tides would require a flawless plan. In the first twelve escape attempts made at Alcatraz, twenty-nine escapees were drowned, shot, or captured. Two escapees were never accounted for, but authorities presumed that they drowned. The thirteenth escape, which took place just a year before Alcatraz closed in 1963, was a sensational blend of improvisation, patience, and bold—or desperate—derring-do. Whether the attempt was a success, however, is a matter of conjecture.

On the Rock

Its proper name is Alcatraz, but the federal prisoners immured on the wave-washed rocky outcropping in San Francisco Bay gave it names more expressive of the spirit of the place: the Tomb of the Living Dead, Hellcatraz, the Rock of Despair, or merely the Rock. At Alcatraz, rehabilitation was unknown, and the regimentation was rigid and unyielding. The toughest of the tough wound up there—fa-

mous gangsters such as Al Capone and Machine Gun Kelly and lesser lights caught before they could earn such dubious glory—bank robbers, murderers, kidnappers, forgers. Tough and street-smart, some-

The principals were three bank robbers, Frank Lee Morris and brothers Clarence and John Anglin. It took months for them to make their preparations, perhaps with the aid of fellow inmates. They squirreled away materials bit by bit—sweepings from the barbershop floor, brushes and paint, glue, scraps of paper. From them the men made several props, including cardboard images of the ventilator grills in their cells. They also improvised papier-mâché and molded it into realistic replicas of their heads, painting the features and gluing on hair sneaked out of the barbershop.

What tools they had is a guess—they may have had nothing more than mess-hall spoons—but under cover of darkness they worked the ventilator grills free, then laboriously scraped away at the concrete walls of the shafts until they were large enough—about ten inches by fourteen inches—to squeeze through. The concrete was deteriorating; had it been in better condition, their plot might have been foiled. During the day their home-made cardboard grills disguised their handiwork.

Through the enlarged ventilator shafts the men clambered up to a space atop the cellblock, where they set up a workshop lit by a flashlight. After lights out, they crept up to fashion life preservers from stolen raincoats. Their workshop also gave them access to an air shaft leading to the roof. Supposedly tool-proof bars had been installed over the shaft's opening, but they yielded to patient prying.

On June 11, Morris and the Anglins were in bed when guards made their routine check immediately after lights out at 9:30. When the coast was clear, the three inmates quickly arranged the dummy heads and the bedclothes so convincingly that when the guards made their rounds later that night they were completely taken in. Speeding up to the roof, the convicts descended the outer wall and pushed off into the bay.

The Anglins and Morris had long since swum or drifted away by the time guards raised the alarm at the morning roll call. Search teams scoured Alcatraz and neighboring Angel Island without success. The only trace of the escapees outside the prison walls was a plastic bag containing a ten-dollar money-order receipt made out to Clarence Anglin and fifty photographs of a woman. The warden speculated that the escapees had perished in the choppy, fifty-four-degree-Fahrenheit waters of San Francisco Bay and been swept through the Golden Gate and out into the Pacific. It was a logical surmise, but to this day, no one can be sure that Frank Morris, Clarence Anglin, and brother John were not the only men ever to escape from the Rock of Despair. □

Old Folks at Home

There is a front porch where old men sit and swap tales. Around about lie clipped hedges, smooth lawns, rose gardens, and private vegetable plots. There is bingo every other Friday, and those who wish can sing in a choir once led by former resident singing star James Brown. You can dress as you like, room and board are free, and so is the first-rate medical care. It is not a bad place—as jails go. Among aging inmates in South Carolina, a transfer from a conven-

tional prison to the comparatively good life of State Park Correctional Center (below) outside Columbia is considered good fortune.

A tuberculosis hospital before it became a facility for aging convicts, State Park is reserved for men and women at least fifty-five years old, unless poor health makes earlier admission advisable. Although the doors are locked at night, officials worry less about security than providing ramps, canes, and walkers for arthritic miscreants. Discipline problems are usually minor. Residents do have their differences, but the favorite method of retaliation among warring gardeners amounts to no more than stripping one another's plots of tomatoes. There is a major incentive to police one's own behavior, since serious troublemakers may wind up in an ordinary prison. One man who stole from his wheelchair-ridden roommate and hit him to boot wound up "under the jail"—in a normal lockup—when the abuse was discovered.

Despite the allure of State Park, some inmates do not wait for parole to taste freedom again. One old inmate tried to escape via a public bus that stopped on the grounds. A chaplain spotted him and foiled his plan. Nevertheless, the man got away on a second try and rode the bus into Columbia. There he celebrated his apparent success in a bar too long and was arrested for public drunkenness. Even though he had two new black marks on his record, State Park took him back. He had a good story for the front porch crowd. □

To cover their escape from seagirt Alcatraz Island, three inmates put papier-mâché likenesses into their beds to fool the guards and delay the alarm (left).

No Smoking

One day in 1982, McKinley Dale Thomas was in bad need of a smoke. So he broke into a Stop N Go convenience store in Houston and stole two cartons of Kools. He got caught.

The prosecuting attorney offered a plea bargain, but Thomas turned it down. And, given the choice between presenting his case to a judge and jury or to a judge alone, he chose a jury trial. Those were two bad calls. The jury sentenced Thomas to the heaviest sentence possible under Texas law—ninety-nine years in jail, along with a $10,000 fine. In terms of cigarettes, the fine alone worked out to $500 a pack. Thomas assessed their action with plaintive understatement: "It doesn't make any sense to give a man ninety-nine years just for some cigarettes."

Simply put, Thomas's problem, according to presiding judge Ted Poe, was that the jury did not like him. They meted out the harsh "piece of Texas justice," the judge said, because of what they perceived as the defendant's volatility, his arrogance, and his contempt for the judicial system. Thomas had a record of convictions for minor offenses. But in the eyes of the jurors, Poe said, the burglar loomed as an "extreme menace," and they threw the book at him.

Even prosecuting attorney Alan Tanner thought the sentence was undeserved, and after Thomas was denied an appeal, the prosecutor himself filed for parole for Thomas. It was granted, but not before Thomas had spent almost eight years behind bars for two cartons of cigarettes. □

A Costly Habit

As Stephen Dennison walked up to a Salem, New York, lunch stand, he wanted a cigarette in the worst way, and he was hungry besides. It was his bad luck that the stand was closed, but he decided to wait for the owner to return. At length his nicotine fit got the better of him, and he took out his jackknife and made a long cut in the stand's canvas cover. Stepping inside, he picked up a carton of cigarettes, some Lifesavers and chocolates, and a silver-toned compact for his mother. He had just lit up when the owner came along and caught him with her compact and five dollars' worth of loot.

Because he was a first-time offender and only sixteen, the judge hearing his case suspended his ten-year sentence to Elmira Reformatory on the conditions that he get a job and meet monthly with the local Methodist minister. Things went swimmingly for the first three months of Dennison's probation. But he could not handle his cigarette craving and was fired from his job for smoking in the men's room. Too humiliated to face the Reverend Winch, Dennison skipped the required meetings and was hauled back into court for violating probation.

The second time around, the judge ordered Dennison to Elmira Reformatory for an indeterminate term. Through some quirk of justice, however, the earlier ten-year sentence went down on the records that accompanied Dennison to the reformatory in 1926.

Elmira had a total ban on smoking, which made life miserable for the addicted youth. When another inmate told him that smoking was permitted at Dannemora State Hospital, Dennison put on a show of madness so convincing that he was transferred from Elmira to complete his sentence on the hospital's psychiatric ward.

When Dennison had served all but one day of his ten-year term, Dannemora officials petitioned the courts to commit him permanently to the hospital, claiming that he was insane. By the time a judge granted the request eight days later, Dennison had more than served his sentence and should have been set free. Neither he nor his family had been notified of the commitment proceedings, however, and no one was poised to go to bat for him. Except for his mother, Dennison had never had visitors, and she had died years earlier. The doors of the mental ward slammed shut, and there Dennison stayed for another quarter of a century.

The miscarriage of justice began to right itself when George, Dennison's half brother, decided it was his duty to pay a visit to Dannemora. A late uncle had willed Stephen $1,300, and George wanted to deliver the news in person, even though hospital officials had claimed Stephen was so ill that he would not recognize family members. On the contrary, Stephen was quite coherent. After hearing his miserable tale of beatings and solitary confinement, George hired a lawyer to investigate the case.

Because Stephen Dennison had been committed to Dannemora without a hearing or legal representation, his attorney won his release on a writ of habeas corpus. After twenty-four years of wrongful confinement, Dennison walked away with his freedom, two pennies that had been in his pocket when he entered Elmira, a suit that was too big for him, and a twenty-dollar check. He lost the check before he had a chance to cash it.

Dennison was awarded $115,000 from New York State for his ordeal, but the judgment was reversed by a higher court. To support himself, he got a job as a janitor and stuck with it. Dennison died, poor but free, in 1991. □

A free man after thirty-four years of confinement, Stephen Dennison enjoys a glass of milk. Dennison's crime was a five-dollar burglary.

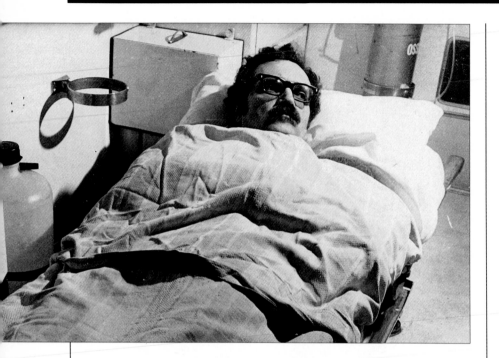

Humdinger

Louis Laslo was about to pull into his Hellertown, Pennsylvania, driveway when the car ahead of his beat him to it. George Reid had intended simply to turn his car around, but the irate Laslo was not going to let him get away with it. Blocking Reid's escape with his own car, Laslo jumped out, snatched Reid's ignition key, and imposed an impromptu sentence: To win his freedom, Reid must hum "Yankee Doodle" while holding his nose and tapping out the rhythm on the steering wheel. Reid's fourteen-year-old son, Laslo decreed, was to hold his own nose throughout the performance.

Vigilante justice left him unsatisfied, and Laslo summoned the police. Neither amused nor sympathetic, they arrested not Reid, but Laslo, and on an alarming assortment of charges: kidnapping, theft, simple assault, terroristic threats, unlawful restraint, and false imprisonment.

Luckily for Laslo, Reid apparently was not a vengeful man. He failed to show up to testify at the trial, and the case was dismissed on September 14, 1989. □

Breaking Down and Out

Mental illness is hardly a welcome disorder, but it can sometimes mean freedom for imprisoned Italians. Under a unique provision of Italy's penal code, a judge may order an inmate's release if confinement triggers a breakdown.

Leave it to the Italians, whose ancestors pioneered the Western world's legal principles, to enact so avant-garde a measure. To be sure, not all convicts with psychiatric disorders can find relief under the sick law. A prisoner convicted of a violent crime need not apply, nor one with a condition that is not severe.

The mental-illness provision was added in 1984 to a law first passed in 1930, which covered organic illnesses and was revolutionary in its time. The original law provides a humanitarian out for convicts

suffering a terminal illness or some chronic malady requiring repeated and protracted hospitalization. Mercy is tempered with justice, however, for fewer than half the applicants go free.

One man whose petition earned the judges' blessing under the new provision was Sergei Antonov, a Bulgarian jailed after the attempted assassination of Pope John Paul II in St. Peter's Square in 1981. Suspected of having driven the gunman to St. Peter's on the day of the shooting, Antonov was imprisoned while he awaited his trial. After a year, he became so profoundly depressed that he was released from jail and placed under house arrest with a police guard at his front door. Finally tried in 1985, he was acquitted and left Italy a free man. □

Flossing to Freedom

Anyone who has dutifully scraped his teeth with dental floss knows that the stuff is tough, but on a November night in 1988 it passed an unconventional strength test with flying colors. One after the other, three prisoners at Manhattan's Metropolitan Correctional Center climbed out a window and slid down a stomach-churning six stories on a floss rope barely one-quarter-inch thick. For a superior grip, they had used the unwaxed variety, buying it from the Center's commissary a roll at a time or bartering for it with other prisoners to avoid arousing suspicion.

The scheme but not the rope was raveling by the time they landed on a third-floor terrace. A guard had already heard them, and they were arrested for trying to escape. There was a technological problem as well. One prisoner, an Iranian jailed for impersonating a U.S. State Department official and for violating federal weapons and explosives laws, was cut so badly by the dental-floss rope that several tendons in his hands were severed and required surgery.

Three years later, a Texas trio apparently unaware of the Manhattan experiment plotted to floss out of the Hays County jail in San Marcos. David Surasky, Arthur Stier, and Ian Holbs were perhaps inspired by the necklaces that fellow inmates braided from dental floss to while away the hours.

The three prisoners were housed in the Tank, a dormitory with a windowed door overlooking a mesh-covered courtyard. To scale its cinder-block walls and reach the ground on the other side, the men set to work on a twenty-foot ladder. For its side pieces, they braided hundreds of yards of dental floss purchased in the handy jail store. Their refined design called for stirruplike steps made of cardboard salt and pepper shakers collected at mealtime and strung on strips of cloth torn from a mattress covering.

With a hacksaw blade smuggled into jail in the sole of a rubber flip-flop, the men attacked the triple-layered Plexiglas window on the night of April 28. They had removed two panes when guards making a bed check spotted the missing panes. Stier blurted out a confession and lifted his mattress to reveal the ladder at the ready.

The other two prisoners stonewalled, but their hands were a dead giveaway—the hard work of sawing had raised a crop of blisters. □

Three prisoners in a Texas jail planned an unsuccessful escape using a hacksaw blade smuggled inside a flip-flop and an ingenious rope ladder that was fashioned from dental floss, salt and pepper shakers, and cloth strips.

ACKNOWLEDGMENTS

The editors wish to thank these individuals and institutions for their valuable assistance in the preparation of this volume:

Judith Harris Ajello, Rome; James R. Badey, Boca Raton, Florida; William Balsamo, Brooklyn; Brigitte Baumbusch, Florence; Paul Begg; Daniele Billitteri, Palermo; Florence Brigham, Fall River Historical Society, Fall River, Massachusetts; Nicolette Bromberg, Kansas Collection, University of Kansas Libraries, Lawrence; Guido Buldrini, ANSA, Rome; William Caruchet, Nice; Sylvie Clair, Conservateur aux Archives d'Outre-mer, Aix-en-Provence; Roderick Conway-Morris, Venice; Carl Johan Cronlund, Polismuseum, Stockholm; Helen Nagge Davis, Marion, Illinois; Gary DeNeal, Harrisburg, Illinois; Olga de Saint Affrique, La Rochelle, France; Franz Dorn, Institut für Rechtsgeschichte, Universität, Bonn; Franco Ferracuti, "La Sapienza"—Università di Roma, Rome; Maria Pia Frangeamore, Istituto di Prevenzione e Pena, Rome; Jonathan Goodman, London; A. C. Greene, Dallas; William Helmer, Chicago; Christoph Hinkledey, Mittelalterliches Kriminalmuseum, Rothenburg; Tamegoro Ikii, Tokyo; Ron Koziol, Chicago Tribune, Homewood, Illinois; Robert Laporte, Mairie de Thiais, Thiais; Norvin Leach, Daily News Mercury, Malden, Massachusetts; Mark Levelle, Chicago; William R. Maples, C. A. Pound Human Identification Laboratory, Florida Museum of Natural History, University of Florida, Gainesville; Fred Martens, Pennsylvania Crime Commission, Conshohocken; Michael Martins, Fall River Historical Society, Fall River, Massachusetts; Milton F. Perry, Clay County Department of Parks, Recreation, and Historic Sites, Division of Historic Research & Development, Liberty, Missouri; Frédéric Pottecher, Paris; Isabelle Sauvé-Astruc, Musée des Collections Historiques de la Préfecture de Police, Paris; Vittorino Scattolon, Rome; David H. Shayt, Smithsonian Institution, Washington, D.C.; Chuck Shepherd, News of the Weird, Washington, D.C.; Görel Söderberg, Informationschef, Polishögskolan, Solna, Sweden; Pierre Veron, Paris; Albert Wills, Cornwell Heights, Pennsylvania; Robert T. Zintl, Rome.

PICTURE CREDITS

The sources for the illustrations that appear in this book are listed below. Credits from left to right are separated by semicolons, from top to bottom by dashes.

Cover: UPI/Bettmann, New York, background, Bruno Barbey/Magnum Photos, New York. **3:** UPI/Bettmann, New York. **7:** The New York Times, New York, background, Four by Five Inc./Superstock, New York. **8:** Fabio Simion Ricciarini, Milan, courtesy Museo Nazionale, Rome. **9:** Jonathan Goodman Collection, London—from Men: A Pictorial Archive from Nineteenth-Century Sources, selected by Jim Harter, Dover Publications, New York, 1980. **10, 11:** Fall River Historical Society, Fall River, Massachusetts (2); © 1990 Martha Swope Photography, New York. **12, 13:** Courtesy Paul Begg, England; from Men: A Pictorial Archive from Nineteenth-Century Sources, selected by Jim Harter, Dover Publications, New York, 1980—the Hulton Picture Company, London. **14:** From Goods and Merchandise: A Cornucopia of Nineteenth-Century Cuts, compiled and arranged by William Rowe, Dover Publications, New York, 1982—Jean-Loup Charmet, Paris, courtesy Musée et Archives de la Préfecture de Police. **15:** From Women: A Pictorial Archive from Nineteenth-Century Sources, selected by Jim Harter, Dover Publications, New York, 1982—Rocky Mountain News, Denver, Colorado. **16:** UPI/Bettmann, New York. **17:** Fort Worth Star-Telegram Photograph Collection, Special Collections Division, the University of Texas at Arlington Libraries, Arlington, Texas—Texas Bankers Association, Austin, Texas. **18:** Art by Time-Life Books—Jonathan Goodman Collection, London (2). **19:** Stockholms Polismuseum, Stockholm. **20, 21:** The Hulton Picture Company, London; Popperfoto, London; published by permission of the Commissioner of the Metropolitan Police, London. **22:** The New York Times, New York. **23:** By permission of the Governors of Dulwich Picture Gallery, London—Blasetti/Ansa, Rome. **24:** Ansa, Rome. **25:** Lassier-Hamelin/Sygma, New York, background, Ledru/Sygma, New York—Doug Menuez, Sausalito, California. **26:** © Ken Biggs/the Stock Market, 1989, New York. **27:** The Daily News-Mercury, Malden, Massachusetts. **28:** Art by Time-Life Books—The Daily News-Mercury, Malden, Massachusetts. **29:** Nashville Banner, Nashville, Tennessee (2). **30:** Nordfoto, Copenhagen. **31:** From Transportation: A Pictorial Archive from Nineteenth-Century Sources, selected by Jim Harter, Dover Publications, New York, 1984—Randy Kermoade/Daily Times-Call, Longmont, Colorado. **32:** Bruce Edwards, Flint Journal, Flint, Michigan; from Treasury of Flower Designs for Artists, Embroiderers and Craftsmen, by Susan Gaber, Dover Publications, New York, 1981. **33:** Evan Sheppard, courtesy Nanci Miller. **35:** The Bettmann Archive, New York, background, Kansas State Historical Society, Topeka, Kansas. **36, 37:** By permission of the British Library, London—from Goods and Merchandise: A Cornucopia of Nineteenth-Century Cuts, compiled and arranged by William Rowe, Dover Publications, New York, 1982; courtesy the Board of Trinity College, Dublin. **38:** Mary Evans Picture Library, London. **39:** Culver Pictures, New York. **40:** Cigna Museum and Art Collection, Philadelphia, Pennsylvania (2). **41:** Culver Pictures, New York (2). **42:** The Bettmann Archive, New York. **43:** Courtesy the Missouri Division of Tourism, Jefferson City, Missouri. **44:** From Machinery and Mechanical Devices: A Treasury of Nineteenth-Century Cuts, selected and arranged by William Rowe, Dover Publications, New York, 1987. **45:** The Kansas State Historical Society, Topeka, Kansas (2). **46, 47:** La Trobe Collection, State Library of Victoria, Melbourne, Victoria, Australia (2). **48:** The Bettmann Archive, New York. **49:** Culver Pictures, New York. **50:** Art by Time-Life Books; from Goods and Merchandise: A Cornucopia of Nineteenth-Century Cuts, compiled and arranged by William Rowe, Dover Publications, New York, 1982—Brown Brothers, Sterling, Pennsylvania (2). **51:** Roger-Viollet, Paris, background, from Transportation: A Pictorial Archive from Nineteenth-Century Sources, selected by Jim Harter, Dover Publications, New York, 1984. **52:** Brown Brothers, Sterling, Pennsylvania. **53:** Courtesy Bill Helmer, Chicago. **54, 55:** UPI/Bettmann, New York (2). **56, 57:** Williamson County Historical Society, Marion, Illinois; UPI/Bettmann, New York (2). **58:** Culver Pictures, New York. **59:** From the Collection of the Henry Ford Museum and Greenfield Village, Dearborn, Michigan. **60:** The Bettmann Archive, New York (2). **61:** David Rogowski, the Journal Newspapers, Springfield, Virginia, courtesy Reta Badey—Alexandra Avakian/Woodfin Camp, New York. **63:** FPG, New York, background, M.

Angelo/Westlight, Los Angeles. **64:** Jean-Loup Charmet, Paris—from *Goods and Merchandise: A Cornucopia of Nineteenth-Century Cuts*, compiled and arranged by William Rowe, Dover Publications, New York, 1982. **65:** Harvard Medical Archives in the Francis A. Countway Library of Medicine, Boston, Massachusetts. **66:** Art by Dan Beisel; art by Time-Life Books. **67:** Courtesy Time Inc. Magazines Picture Collection, New York. **68:** Culver Pictures, New York (2). **69:** The Bettmann Archive, New York. **70:** Syndication International, London—from *Ready-to-Use, Old-Fashioned Transportation Cuts*, edited by Carol Belanger Grafton, Dover Publications, New York, 1987; Syndication International, London. **71:** Wide World Photos, New York. **72:** FPG, New York—UPI/Bettmann, New York. **73:** UPI/Bettmann, New York. **74:** Special Collections and Archives, Rutgers University Libraries, New Brunswick, New Jersey—from *Animals: A Pictorial Archive from Nineteenth-Century Sources*, selected by Jim Harter, Dover Publications, New York, 1979. **75:** From *Goods and Merchandise: A Cornucopia of Nineteenth-Century Cuts*, compiled and arranged by William Rowe, Dover Publications, New York, 1982. **76:** Art by Time-Life Books—Archives Tallandier, Paris; from *Goods and Merchandise: A Cornucopia of Nineteenth-Century Cuts*, compiled and arranged by William Rowe, Dover Publications, New York, 1982. **77:** Yomiuri Shimbun, Tokyo. **78:** The Bettmann Archive, New York. **79:** Associated Press Photo, New York, background, from *Treasury of Flower Designs for Artists, Embroiderers and Craftsmen*, by Susan Gaber, Dover Publications, New York, 1981. **80:** Wide World Photos, New York. **81:** *The Miami Herald*, Miami. **83:** Wide World Photos, New York. **84:** AP/Wide World, New York. **85:** Art by Time-Life Books—*The Washington Star*, courtesy the Washingtoniana Division of the Martin Luther King, Jr., Library, Washington, D.C. (2). **87:** Mike Salisbury, background, W. Cody/Westlight, Los Angeles. **88:** Library of Congress LC-109553. **89:** Research Division, Department of Library, Archives, and Public Records, State of Arizona, Phoenix (2). **90:** AP/Wide World Photos, New York. **91:** Art by Time-Life Books. **92, 93:** UPI/Bettmann, New York (2). **94:** Courtesy of the Andry Montgomery Collection, London; UPI/Bettmann, New York. **95:** Art by Time-Life Books. **96, 97:** UPI/Bettmann, New York; David Seymour/Magnum Photos Inc., New York. **99:** UPI/Bettmann, New York. **100:** From *Goods and Merchandise: A Cornucopia of Nineteenth-Century Cuts*, compiled and arranged by William Rowe, Dover Publications, New York, 1982. **101:** Agence France Presse, Paris. **102, 103:** UPI/Bettmann, New York (2). **104:** Sandy Porter/*Sunday Times*, London—AP/Wide World Photos, New York; Mike Salisbury. **105:** Murray Alcosser/the Image Bank, New York. **106:** Murray Alcosser/the Image Bank, New York; Lizzie Himmel/Sygma, New York. **107:** Library of Congress LC-14621, background, M. Stephenson/Westlight, Los Angeles. **108:** The American School of Classical Studies, Athens, Greece. **109:** J&M Photographes, La Rochelle. **110:** Jean-Loup Charmet, Paris. **111:** Scala, Florence. **112:** Jean-Loup Charmet, Paris. **113:** Edimedia, Paris; from *Weapons and Armour: A Pictorial Archive of Woodcuts and Engravings*, edited by Harold H. Hart, Dover Publications, New York, 1978. **114:** Art by Time-Life Books—Library of Congress HV8519.M3, Rare Book Collection. **115:** Mansell Collection, London—UPI/Bettmann, New York. **116:** Mary Evans Picture Library, London. **117:** Petherick Collection, National Library of Australia, Canberra. **118:** *Illustrated London News* Picture Library, London. **119:** National Museum of American History, Smithsonian Institution, 88-6059-27A. **120:** Board of Trustees of the Royal Armouries, London, Class XV-5—Mary Evans Picture Library, London; Mittelalterliches Kriminalmuseum, Rothenburg, Germany (2). **121:** Mittelalterliches Kriminalmuseum, Rothenburg, Germany (2)—Mary Evans Picture Library, London. **122:** Gianni Dagli Orti, Paris—Mary Evans Picture Library, London—Mittelalterliches Kriminalmuseum, Rothenburg, Germany. **123:** Mary Evans Picture Library, London; Scala, Florence. **124:** Library of Congress LC-14621. **125:** The Hulton Picture Company, London (2). **126:** Art by Time-Life Books. **127:** Roger-Viollet, Paris. **128:** Jim McHugh/*LIFE* (3), background, John Stampfli/National Park Service, Washington, D.C. **129:** Courtesy South Carolina Department of Corrections, Columbia, South Carolina. **130:** Texas Department of Criminal Justice, Huntsville Prison, Texas—from *Men: A Pictorial Archive from Nineteenth-Century Sources*, selected by Jim Harter, Dover Publications, New York, 1980. **131:** Lisa Hoffmann, Southbury, Connecticut. **132:** Ansa, Rome—adapted from a drawing from Culver Pictures, New York. **133:** Art by Time-Life Books—Peter A. Silva/Picture Group, Providence, Rhode Island.

BIBLIOGRAPHY

Books

The American Prison. College Park, Md.: The American Correctional Association, 1983.

Andrews, William. *Old-Time Punishments*. Williamstown, Mass.: Corner House, 1977.

Angle, Paul M. *Bloody Williamson*. New York: Alfred A. Knopf, 1952.

Asbury, Herbert:
The Gangs of New York. Garden City, N.Y.: Garden City Publishing, 1928.
Gem of the Prairie. DeKalb, Ill.: Northern Illinois University Press, 1986.
Gem of the Prairie. New York: Alfred A. Knopf, 1940.

Balsamo, William, and George Carpozi, Jr. *Under the Clock*. Far Hills, N.J.: New Horizon Press, 1988.

Black, Charles, and Michael Horsnell. *Counterfeiter: The Story of a British Master Forger*. London: Hodder & Stoughton, New English Library, 1989.

Bloom, Murray Teigh. *The Man Who Stole Portugal*. London: Secker & Warburg, 1953.

Boehm, David A. (Ed.). *Daring Rascals*. New York: Sterling, 1986.

Borchard, Edwin M. *Convicting the Innocent*. Garden City, N.Y.: Garden City Publishing, 1932.

Burt, Olive Woolley (Ed.). *American Murder Ballads and Their Stories*. New York: Oxford University Press, 1958.

Camp, John M. *The Athenian Agora*. London: Thames & Hudson, 1986.

Churchill, Allen. *A Pictorial History of American Crime, 1849-1929*. New York: Holt, Rinehart & Winston, 1964.

Cohen, Daniel. *The Encyclopedia of Unsolved Crimes*. New York: Dodd, Mead, 1988.

Crimes and Punishment (Vol. 8). New York: Marshall Cavendish, 1986.

Criminal Justice through the Ages (Vol. 4). Translated by John Fosberry. Rothenburg ob der Tauber, Germany: Mediaeval Crime Museum, 1981.

Crivello, Kirk. *Fallen Angels*. Secaucus, N.J.: Citadel Press, 1988.

Crosbie, John S. *The Incredible Mrs. Chadwick*. Toronto: McGraw-Hill Ryerson, 1975.

Davis, Allen F., and Mark H. Haller (Eds.). *The*

Peoples of Philadelphia: A History of Ethnic Groups and Lower-Class Life, 1790-1940. Philadelphia: Temple University Press, 1973.

Deeson, A. F. L. *Great Swindlers.* New York: Drake, 1972.

DeNeal, Gary. *A Knight of Another Sort.* Danville, Ill.: Interstate Printers & Publishers, 1981.

Dew, Walter. *I Caught Crippen.* London: Blackie & Son, 1938.

Earle, Alice Morse. *Curious Punishments of Bygone Days.* Montclair, N.J.: Patterson Smith, 1969 (reprint of 1896 edition).

Edgerton, Samuel Y., Jr. *Pictures and Punishment: Art and Criminal Prosecution during the Florentine Renaissance.* Ithaca, N.Y.: Cornell University Press, 1985.

Eldridge, Benj. P., and William B. Watts. *Our Rival the Rascal.* Boston: Pemberton, 1897.

Ellis, John. *The Social History of the Machine Gun.* Baltimore: Johns Hopkins University Press, 1986.

Feder, Sid, Edward Gibbons, and Joseph F. Dinneen. *The Great Brink's Holdup.* Garden City, N.Y.: Doubleday, 1961.

Finger, Charles J. *Highwaymen: A Book of Gallant Rogues.* Freeport, N.Y.: Books for Libraries Press, 1970 (reprint of 1923 edition).

Fisher, Jim. *The Lindbergh Case.* New Brunswick, N.J.: Rutgers University Press, 1987.

Freeman, Lucy, and Lisa Hoffman. *The Ordeal of Stephen Dennison.* Englewood Cliffs, N.J.: Prentice-Hall, 1970.

Garrett, Richard. *Hoaxes and Swindles.* London: Severn House, 1979.

Gatton, T. Harry. *The Texas Bankers Association: The First Century, 1885-1985.* Austin: Texas Bankers Association, 1984.

Gaute, J. H. H., and Robin Odell. *The Murderers' Who's Who.* New York: Methuen, 1979.

Gentry, Curt. *The Vulnerable Americans.* Garden City, N.Y.: Doubleday, 1966.

Gettinger, Stephen H. *Sentenced to Die.* New York: Macmillan, 1979.

Gibson, Walter B. (Ed.). *The Fine Art of Swindling.* New York: Grosset & Dunlap, 1966.

Goodman, Jonathan. *The Slaying of Joseph Bowne Elwell.* New York: St. Martin's Press, 1987.

Graves, Robert. *The Twelve Caesars.* New York: Penguin Books, 1957.

Greene, A. C.:
The Santa Claus Bank Robbery. Austin, Tex.: Texas Monthly Press, 1972.
The Santa Claus Bank Robbery. Cisco, Tex.: Longhorn Press, 1958.

Grombach, John V. *The Great Liquidator.* Garden City, N.Y.: Doubleday, 1980.

Hartman, Mary S. *Victorian Murderesses.* New York: Schocken Books, 1977.

Haskins, James. *Street Gangs: Yesterday and Today.* New York: Hastings House, 1974.

Healey, Tim. *The World's Greatest Crimes of Passion.* New York: Berkley Books, 1985.

Helmer, William J. *The Gun That Made the Twenties Roar.* London: Collier-Macmillan, 1969.

Hibbert, Christopher. *The Roots of Evil.* Boston: Little, Brown, 1963.

Higdon, Hal. *The Crime of the Century.* New York: G. P. Putnam's Sons, 1975.

Hill, E. Bishop. *Complete History of the Southern Illinois Gang War.* Harrisburg, Ill.: Hill, 1927.

Honeycombe, Gordon. *The Murders of the Black Museum.* London: Hutchinson, 1982.

Hughes, Robert. *The Fatal Shore.* New York: Alfred A. Knopf, 1987.

Infamous Murders. Secaucus, N.J: Book Sales, Chartwell Books, 1989.

Ives, George. *A History of Penal Methods: Criminals, Witches, Lunatics.* London: Stanley Paul, 1970.

Jennings, Dean. *We Only Kill Each Other: The Life and Bad Times of Bugsy Siegel.* Englewood Cliffs, N.J.: Prentice-Hall, 1967.

Johnson, David R. *Policing the Urban Underworld.* Philadelphia: Temple University Press, 1979.

Johnson, Robert. *Death Work: A Study of the Modern Execution Process.* Pacific Grove, Calif.: Wadsworth, Brooks/Cole, 1990.

Jones, Ann. *Women Who Kill.* New York: Holt Rinehart & Winston, 1980.

Jones, Steve. *London: The Sinister Side.* London: Tragical History Tours, 1986.

Joselit, Jenna Weissman. *Our Gang.* Bloomington, Ind.: Indiana University Press, 1983.

Kadish, Sanford H. (Ed.). *Encyclopedia of Crime and Justice* (Vol. 3). New York: Macmillan, Free Press, 1983.

Keating, H. R. F. *Great Crimes.* New York: Harmony Books, 1982.

Kent, Arthur. *Deadly Medicine.* New York: Taplinger, 1975.

Klausner, Lawrence D. *Son of Sam.* New York: McGraw-Hill, 1981.

Klein, Alexander (Ed.):
The Double Dealers. Philadelphia: J. B. Lippincott, 1958.
Grand Deception. Philadelphia: J. B. Lippincott, 1955.

Lagrange, Francis, and William Murray. *Flag on Devil's Island.* Garden City, N.Y.: Doubleday, 1961.

McKelvey, Blake. *American Prisons: A History of Good Intentions.* Montclair, N.J.: Patterson Smith, 1977.

Martin, John Bartlow. *Butcher's Dozen: And Other Murders.* New York: Harper & Brothers, 1950.

Mason, George Henry. *The Punishments of China.* London: William Miller, 1808.

Maurer, David W. *The American Confidence Man.* Springfield, Ill.: Charles C Thomas, 1974.

Meredith, John, and Bill Scott. *Ned Kelly: After a Century of Acrimony.* Dee Why West, New South Wales, Australia: Lansdowne Press, 1980.

Messick, Hank. *Secret File.* New York: G. P. Putnam's Sons, 1969.

Messick, Hank, and Burt Goldblatt:
Gangs and Gangsters. New York: Ballantine Books, 1974.
The Mobs and the Mafia. New York: Thomas Y. Crowell, 1972.

Miles, Alexander. *Devil's Island.* Berkeley, Calif.: Ten Speed Press, 1988.

Miller, Arthur S., and Jeffrey H. Bowman. *Death by Installments: The Ordeal of Willie Francis.* Westport, Conn.: Greenwood Press, 1988.

Miller, Norman C. *The Great Salad Oil Swindle.* New York: Coward McCann, 1965.

Morain, Alfred. *The Underworld of Paris.* New York: E. P. Dutton, 1931.

Mossiker, Frances. *The Affair of the Poisons.* New York: Alfred A. Knopf, 1969.

Murray, George. *The Legacy of Al Capone.* New York: G. P. Putnam's Sons, 1975.

Nash, Jay Robert:
Encyclopedia of World Crime (4 vols.). Wilmette, Ill.: Crime Books, 1989 and 1990.
Look for the Woman. New York: M. Evans, 1981.
Murder among the Mighty. New York: Delacorte Press, 1983.
Open Files. New York: McGraw-Hill, 1983.

Nixon, Allan M. *100 Australian Bushrangers, 1789-1901.* Adelaide, Australia: Rigby, 1982.

Peterson, Virgil W. *The Mob.* Ottawa, Ill.: Green Hill, 1983.

Powell, Donald M. *The Peralta Grant.* Norman, Okla.: University of Oklahoma Press, 1960.

Rickard, Graham. *Prisons and Punishment.* New York: Bookwright Press, 1987.

Rickards, Colin. *The Man from Devil's Island.* New York: Stein & Day, 1968.

Rose, Colin (Ed.). *The World's Greatest Rip-Offs.* New York: Sterling, 1978.

Ross, Christian K. *The Father's Story of Charley Ross, the Kidnapped Child.* Philadelphia: John E. Potter, 1876.

Roughead, W. N. *Classic Crimes.* New York: Random House, Vintage Books, 1977.

Scharf, J. Thomas, and Thompson Westcott. *History of Philadelphia, 1609-1884* (Vol. 3). Philadelphia: I. H. Everts, 1884.

Scoundrels and Scalawags. Pleasantville, N.Y.: Reader's Digest Association, 1968.

Shaplen, Robert. *Kreuger: Genius and Swindler.* New York: Garland, 1986.

Sifakis, Carl:

The Encyclopedia of American Crime. New York: Facts On File, 1982.

The Mafia Encyclopedia. New York: Facts On File, 1987.

Simpson, Keith. *Forty Years of Murder.* New York: Charles Scribner's Sons, 1979.

Simpson, William R., Florence K. Simpson, and Charles Samuels. *Hockshop.* New York: Random House, 1954.

Sullivan, Robert. *The Disappearance of Dr. Parkman.* Boston: Little, Brown, 1971.

Symons, Julian. *Crime and Detection: An Illustrated History from 1840.* London: Studio Vista, 1966.

Thompson, Erwin N. *The Rock: A History of Alcatraz Island, 1847-1972.* Denver, Colo.: National Park Service, United States Department of the Interior, 1979.

Thompson, Stansbury. *The Story of Jenny Diver.* London: Arthur H. Stockwell, 1940.

Train, John. *Famous Financial Fiascos.* New York: Clarkson N. Potter, 1985.

Treherne, J. E. *The Strange History of Bonnie and Clyde.* New York: Stein & Day, 1985.

Triplett, William. *Flowering of the Bamboo.* Kensington, Md.: Woodbine House, 1985.

van Dülmen, Richard. *Theatre of Horror: Crime and Punishment in Early Modern Germany.* Cambridge: Polity Press, 1990.

Vincent, Arthur (Ed.). *Lives of Twelve Bad Women.* London: T. Fisher Unwin, 1897.

Wade, Carlson. *Great Hoaxes and Famous Impostors.* Middle Village, N.Y.: Jonathan David, 1976.

Walker, Peter N. *Punishment: An Illustrated History.* Newton Abbot, Devon: David & Charles, 1972.

Wallechinsky, David, and Irving Wallace. *The People's Almanac.* Garden City, N.Y.: Doubleday, 1975.

Wellman, Paul I. *A Dynasty of Western Outlaws.* New York: Crown, Bonanza Books, 1961.

Whiting, Roger. *Crime and Punishment: A Study across Time.* Leckhampton, Cheltenham: Stanley Thornes, 1986.

Wilson, Colin, and Damon Wilson. *The Encyclopedia of Unsolved Mysteries.* Chicago: Contemporary Books, 1988.

Wooldridge, Clifton R. *Hands Up!* Chicago: Chicago Police, 1901.

Zierold, Norman. *Little Charley Ross.* Boston: Little, Brown, 1967.

Periodicals

Bainbridge, J. S., Jr. "Devil's Island Is Still a Synonym for Hell on Earth." *Smithsonian,* August 1988.

Barrett, George. "Theft at Tiffany 5th in 121 Years." *New York Times,* August 11, 1958.

"Bodies of Five Slain Unearthed in Yard." *New York Times,* May 6, 1908.

Cartledge, Paul. "The Athenian State Prison." *History Today,* March 1990.

Cody, Edward. "France Will Retire Its Guillotine and Abolish the Death Penalty." *Washington Post,* September 18, 1981.

"Cripple Admits Guilt; Tells How He Carried Gold in Artificial Leg." *Rocky Mountain News,* February 6, 1920.

Crist, Judith. "Tiffany Loot May Be Hard to Sell." *New York Herald Tribune,* August 12, 1958.

Dibbets, Hiske. "Going to the Dogs." *Moscow Magazine,* September 1990.

"'Doctor, Doctor, I Need Help.'" *The News* (Portsmouth), December 2, 1981.

Duplay, Maurice. "La Bande A Bonnot." *Historia,* December 1961.

"Elephant Executing a Criminal at Baroda." *The Illustrated Sporting and Dramatic News,* December 4, 1875.

Elliott, Keith. "The Santa Claus Robbery." *Texas Parade,* December 1965.

"Exit the Bobbed-Haired Bandit—Twenty Years." *Literary Digest,* May 24, 1924.

Farrell, Mary H. J., and Maria Wilhelm. "Armed with a White Cane, Sightless Robert Toye Tapped His Way to the Teller and Robbed 17 Banks Blind." *People,* December 10, 1990.

Fisher, Matthew. "Soviet Motorcycle Gangs: Rebels without Wheels." *Lawrence Eagle-Tribune,* September 25, 1989.

"Flossed and Found." *Time,* July 1, 1991.

"Fourth Filch." *Time,* June 13, 1983.

Gates, Kathy:

"Family's Teamwork Leads to Capture." *Longmont Times-Call,* March 30, 1989.

"Kelm Linked to 8 Robberies." *Longmont Times-Call,* March 31, 1989.

"Suspect Had Many Brushes with Law." *Longmont Times-Call,* March 30, 1989.

Hagedorn, Ann:

"By Gum, This Certainly Wasn't Your Usual Brush with the Law." *Wall Street Journal,* August 11, 1989.

"Geriatric Convicts Get Prison with Raps and Rails and Tomato-Plant Fights." *Wall Street Journal,* September 19, 1989.

Hass, Ted. "Chambersburg Man Forced to Hum Song." *Public Opinion,* April 21, 1989.

Helmer, William J. "Evil Weapon Arms Gangs." *Chicago,* March 1990.

Hyde, Walter Woodburn. "Lifeless Things and Animals in Greek Law." *American Journal of Philology,* April-June 1917.

"Jailed for Life, Southsea Man a Psychopath." *The News* (Portsmouth), February 2, 1981.

Kelland, Clarence B. "The Red Baron of Arizona." *Saturday Evening Post,* October 11, 1947.

Knight, Althelia, and Janet Cooke. "Prison Escapee Charged with Slaying of Dr. Halberstam." *Washington Post,* December 7, 1980.

Kramer, Evelynne. "Lizzie Borden: A Way of Leading Students to the Cutting Edge of Historical Analysis." *University Bulletin,* April 25, 1974.

Laporte, Robert. "La 'Bande A Bonnot' a Thiais." *La Gazette de Thiais,* June 1987-April 1988.

Levey, Robert. "The Boot Man Meets His Match." *Washington Post,* February 12, 1991.

"Life Jail Sentence despite Plea for Hospital." *The News* (Portsmouth), February 12, 1981.

Loggins, Kirk:

"Jury Condemns Terry to Death by Electrocution." *Daily Tennessean,* September 26, 1988.

"'Saw Enough' to Doubt Body Terry's: Police." *Daily Tennessean,* September 20, 1988.

"Terry ID Ruse 'Painful,' Witness Testifies." *Daily Tennessean,* September 21, 1988.

"Terry 'Suicide' Became Murder." *Daily Tennessean,* September 23, 1988.

"Terry's Wife 'Just Glad to See Him.'" *Daily Tennessean,* September 24, 1988.

McCullough, Leslie:

"Tearful Terry Admits Murder." *Tennessee Banner,* September 22, 1988.

"Terry Paid Lawyer Fees with Motorcycle, Wife Says." *Tennessee Banner,* September 24, 1988.

McNamara, Joe. "Murder for a Penny." *Daily News* (New York), January 15, 1984.

"Man Gets 99-Year Term in Burglary of Stop N Go." *Houston Chronicle,* August 11, 1982.

"The Man with the Golden Leg." *Empire Magazine,* November 13, 1966.

Maraniss, David. "'Eccentric' Is Suspect in Rare Book Thefts." *Washington Post,* April 1, 1990.

Miller, Norman C. "How Phantom Salad Oil Was Used to Engineer $100 Million Swindle." *Wall Street Journal,* December 2, 1963.

"Never Too Old for a Heist." *Time,* April 17, 1989.

"Of Fan Mail, Criminals, and Fords." *American Archivist,* Fall 1987.

Osher, Chris. "Witness: Blumberg, Fascinated by Antiques, 'Created Own World.'" *Des Moines Register,* January 30, 1991.

Pelleck, Carl J. "Cops Searching for 'Inside Man' in 163G Tiffany Window Robbery." *New York Post,* August 11, 1958.

Pelton, Robert. "Orville and the Golden Fleece." *The American West,* Fall 1990.

"Prisoners." *Time,* March 25, 1966.

"Pushing His Luck—and His Blood Pressure—

an Aged Bank Robber Is Caught Red-Handed." *People*, April 17, 1989.

Read, Jan. "Image of Terry as Cold-Blooded Stuns Parishioners." *Tennessee Banner*, September 10, 1988.

"Sam Changed after LSD Trips." *Daily News* (New York), August 12, 1977.

"The Secret Art of Making Money." *Sunday Times* (London), June 10, 1990.

Shayt, David H. "Stairway to Redemption: America's Encounter with the British Prison Tread-mill." *Technology and Culture*, October 1989.

Shriner, Dan:
    "Here Comes Bride for Narc Sting." *Flint Journal*, September 22, 1990.
    "Sting Idea Began with Bottles, Cans." *Flint Journal*, September 23, 1990.

Simpson, Colin. "The Berenson Scandals." *Connoisseur*, October 1986.

Smothers, Ronald. "Jailed for Paddling the Paddler." *New York Times*, November 13, 1987.

Willey, Fay, and Elizabeth Peer. "To Lose a Thief." *Newsweek*, March 21, 1977.

"Wooden Leg Used to Transport Stolen Bullion." *Rocky Mountain News*, December 26, 1982.

"'Yankee Doodle' Order Leads to Jail." *Morning Call*, April 20, 1989.

Other

Thomas, McKinley. "Junk Bonds/Junk Justice." Interviewed by Steve Dunleavy, May 30, 1990. Current Affair, Fox Television.

INDEX

Time-Life Books is a division of Time Life Inc., a wholly owned subsidiary of **THE TIME INC. BOOK COMPANY**

TIME-LIFE BOOKS

Managing Editor: Thomas H. Flaherty
Director of Editorial Resources:
Elise D. Ritter-Clough
Director of Photography and Research:
John Conrad Weiser
Editorial Board: Dale M. Brown, Roberta Conlan, Laura Foreman, Lee Hassig, Jim Hicks, Blaine Marshall, Rita Thievon Mullin, Henry Woodhead

Associate Publisher: Ann M. Mirabito
Editorial Director: Russell B. Adams, Jr.
Marketing Director: Anne C. Everhart
Production Manager: Prudence G. Harris
Supervisor of Quality Control: James King

Editorial Operations
Production: Celia Beattie
Library: Louise D. Forstall
Computer Composition: Deborah G. Tait (Manager), Monika D. Thayer, Janet Barnes Syring, Lillian Daniels

Library of Congress Cataloging-in-Publication Data
Crimes and punishments / by the editors of Time-Life Books.
p. cm. (Library of curious and unusual facts).
Includes bibliographical references.
ISBN 0-8094-7727-0 (trade)
ISBN 0-8094-7728-9 (lib. bdg.)
1. Crime—Miscellanea. 2. Punishment—Miscellanea.
I. Time-Life Books. II. Series.
HV6233.C7 1991
364—dc20   91-22777 CIP

LIBRARY OF CURIOUS AND UNUSUAL FACTS

SERIES EDITOR: Laura Foreman
Series Administrator: Roxie France-Nuriddin
Art Director: Cynthia Richardson
Picture Editor: Catherine M. Chase

Editorial Staff for *Crimes and Punishments*
Text Editors: John R. Sullivan (principal), Sarah Brash
Associate Editor/Research: Susan E. Arritt (principal)
Assistant Editors/Research: Michael E. Howard, Ruth J. Moss
Assistant Art Director: Alan Pitts
Senior Copy Coordinators: Jarelle S. Stein (principal), Anthony K. Pordes
Picture Coordinator: Jennifer Iker
Editorial Assistant: Terry Ann Paredes

Special Contributors: Tony Allan, John Clausen, George Constable, Bonnie Gordon, Gina Maranto, Leslie Marshall (text); Libby Schleichert (text and research); Andra H. Armstrong, Ellen C. Gross, Tanya Nádas-Taylor (research); Louise Wile (index)

Correspondents: Elisabeth Kraemer-Singh (Bonn), Christine Hinze (London), Christina Lieberman (New York), Maria Vincenza Aloisi (Paris), Ann Natanson (Rome).
Valuable assistance was also provided by Barbara Mirka Gondicas (Athens); Gevene Hertz (Copenhagen); Caroline Alcock, Judy Aspinall (London); Trini Bandrés (Madrid); Constance Richards (Moscow); Elizabeth Brown, Katheryn White (New York); Leonora Dodsworth, Ann Wise (Rome); Mary Johnson (Stockholm); Dick Berry, Mieko Ikeda (Tokyo).

The Consultants:
William R. Corliss, the general consultant for the series, is a physicist-turned-writer who has spent the last twenty-five years compiling collections of anomalies in the fields of geophysics, geology, archaeology, astronomy, biology, and psychology. He has written about science and technology for NASA, the National Science Foundation, and the Energy Research and Development Administration (among others). Mr. Corliss is also the author of more than thirty books on scientific mysteries, including *Mysterious Universe, The Unfathomed Mind,* and *Handbook of Unusual Natural Phenomena.*

David R. Johnson is a professor of history in the Division of Behavioral and Cultural Sciences at the University of Texas at San Antonio. He is the author of three books: *Policing the Urban Underworld: The Impact of Crimes on the Development of the Police in America, 1800-1887; American Law Enforcement: A History;* and *The Politics of San Antonio: Community, Progress, and Power.*